Happy Knitter
VARIETY PUZZLES

Lindsay Conner

60+ Large-Print Word Puzzles
for Yarn Lovers

C&T PUBLISHING
Another Maker Inspired!

Contents

Instructions 4

PUZZLES

PRODUCT TEAM: Lindsay Conner, Betsy La Honta, Julie Creus, April Mostek, Zinnia Heinzmann, and Jennifer Warren

10 9 8 7 6 5 4 3 2 1

Instructions

 ## Word Mines

See how many words you can make out of the letters in popular yarn types!

⎡ YARN TYPES ⎤

WOOL

3-letter words (4)

L O O

L O W

O W L

W O O

2-letter words (8)

L O

O W

W O

 ## Word RoundUps™

Word RoundUps are a combination of traditional word searches and crossword puzzles. Use the crossword-style clues to identify the hidden words.

WORD ROUNDUP SAMPLE

 3 tools knitters use regularly

 2 knit stitches that double as plants

Word Scrambles

Who doesn't love a good word scramble? Unscramble the letters to find words that match the scramble's theme.

GIDNOI . . . . .indigo

RWPOED BULE . . . . .powder blue

VYNA . . . . .navy

DHMTIIGN . . . . .midnight

 # Criss Crosses

Like Word RoundUps, Criss Cross puzzles are a combination of word searches and crossword puzzles. The grid is like a crossword puzzle, but instead of clues, the words are listed as they are in a word search. Fill the words into their spots in the puzzle, guided by the placement of letters where words cross. The easiest way to get started is to place words where there is only one option (for example, if there is only one word with three letters). If there aren't any of those, start with a letter grouping with few entries and compare crossing words.

CRAFTER'S ACTIVITIES

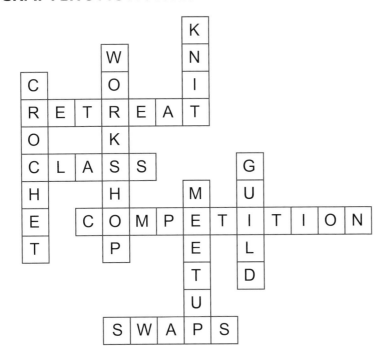

11 letters
COMPETITION

8 letters
WORKSHOP

7 letters
CROCHET
RETREAT

6 letters
MEETUP

5 letters
GUILD
SWAPS
CLASS

4 letters
KNIT

Logic Puzzles

Each logic puzzle is a simple story involving different elements, such as people, places, things, times, and amounts. Your goal in solving a logic puzzle is to figure out the relationship between the different elements. Each logic puzzle has a little background on the story and a list of clues. It's also accompanied by a grid that you can use to help solve the puzzle.

*Read through the clues. Each time you learn that two elements are or are not related, record the fact in the grid. If the fact is something that is **NOT TRUE** (that Rufus is not 8 years old, for example), use an **X** in the grid. If the fact is **TRUE** (that Rufus is wearing the cable-knit sweater), use an **O** in the grid. Use your deductive reasoning to eliminate options. In clue 1 below, for example, you know that Rufus is not 8 years old. You also know that the 8-year-old dog is wearing the reindeer hoodie so Rufus could not be wearing the hoodie.*

Work through the puzzle in blocks of related facts. When you eliminate all but one possibility for an element in a block, you know that remaining possibility is the correct answer, and you can X out other possibilities for that element.

Each positive answer will lead to more related facts, and you will deduce your way to solving the puzzle!

DOGGIE COATS

Four dogs got some knit winterwear from their crafty owners. Figure out which pet is wearing which item, as well as the pets' ages.

1. Rufus is wearing the cable-knit sweater, but is not 8 years old.

2. The dog with the wool socks is 2 years younger than Chloe.

3. King is either 7 or 9 years old.

4. The 8-year-old dog is wearing the reindeer hoodie.

5. Sadie did not wear the socks.

		OUTERWEAR				AGE			
		Cable-knit sweater	Reindeer hoodie	Snowflake hat	Wool socks	7 years	8 years	9 years	10 years
DOG	Rufus	O	X	X	X		X		
	King	X					X		X
	Sadie	X			X				
	Chloe	X			X	X	X		
AGE	7 years		X						
	8 years	X	O	X	X				
	9 years		X		X				
	10 years		X		X				

DOG	OUTERWEAR	AGE
Rufus	Cable-knit sweater	
King		
Sadie		
Chloe		

 # Crossword Puzzles

Solve the clues and enter your answers into the puzzle boxes, following the clue number and word orientation.

 # Word Searches

Look for the words in the word list in the puzzle. Words can run forward, backward, up, down, and on any diagonal.

Puzzles

Crossword Puzzle 1

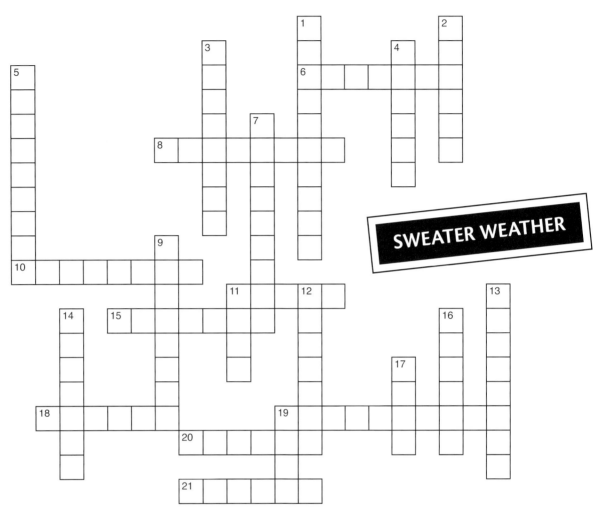

SWEATER WEATHER

ACROSS

6 vertical stripes used on cuffs

8 sweater with no front opening

10 Mr. Rogers wore a red one

11 reveals the decolletage (2 wds)

15 Freddy Krueger's shirt pattern

18 use drawstrings to adjust this

19 covers arms completely (2 wds)

20 shoulder seams run across the chest

21 not gender specific

DOWN

1 style worn by Steve Jobs or Velma (2 wds)

2 diamond plaid

3 one piece that's knit in the round (2 wds)

4 YKK

5 sweater measurement diagram

7 beau

9 Scottish island famous for multicolored knits (2 wds)

11 sleeveless, studious look

12 Charlie Brown style and 2010 trend

13 like many Hanes tees

14 round fasteners

16 sweater, to a Brit

17 some Christmas sweaters are

19 open knit known for eyelets

Word Search 1

AMIGURUMI

```
J  H  F  D  D  K  V  Q  Y  O  U  B  K  A  W  A  I  I  A  K
G  E  Q  R  K  I  D  I  I  X  Y  N  M  I  Z  F  O  C  G  Z
S  D  L  E  U  H  O  I  Z  J  V  O  T  E  E  F  F  O  C  B
A  U  E  L  B  I  G  M  N  Y  N  J  S  K  E  Z  W  T  A  C
Z  G  S  F  Y  F  T  I  P  S  L  L  O  D  O  O  D  O  O  V
Z  Q  D  H  X  F  V  S  T  Z  N  R  A  E  B  Y  D  D  E  T
I  Z  I  O  I  B  I  E  R  T  J  J  R  U  A  S  O  N  I  D
P  R  O  L  L  B  R  S  G  U  L  T  N  E  L  U  C  C  U  S
V  M  V  M  M  L  A  J  H  G  Y  B  Q  Y  U  N  X  Y  D  O
Z  I  H  P  B  B  Y  H  Q  W  I  Q  J  S  V  X  U  H  B  N
U  W  H  M  E  I  E  G  N  M  R  E  C  U  V  V  T  Y  I  R
Z  J  C  D  G  L  E  L  S  E  M  T  S  P  A  O  C  E  R  O
R  S  E  L  K  J  Q  A  W  D  X  Q  Q  O  L  T  H  K  D  C
F  O  X  C  E  N  Q  O  S  Z  L  Q  P  T  Z  J  X  N  G  I
R  I  I  T  I  U  L  T  U  N  O  D  P  C  L  A  F  O  D  N
W  P  M  Y  H  F  I  L  J  C  D  W  Z  O  Z  D  R  M  S  U
```

BIRD	FOX	PIZZA
CAT	FRUITS	SUCCULENT
COFFEE	JELLYFISH	SUSHI
DINOSAUR	KAWAII	TEDDY BEAR
DOG	MONKEY	UNICORN
DOLL	MONSTER	VEGGIES
DONUT	OCTOPUS	VOODOO DOLL
FLOWER	PICKLE	ZOMBIE

Word Search 2

CELEBS WHO KNIT OR CROCHET

```
K A T H E R I N E H E I G L R P K H G O
K P I U A Y G R A C E K E L L Y I J H D
J E F A K A T Y P E R R Y W T H G X E E
T Q D N A L Y S S A M I L A N O Z B T V
K H O I M B E T T E D A V I S G R R E A
D H O L G L V R D X W A B Y J A A T T L
H N W K H N Q T P H B E O K M N T P Y O
E E R N T N J E O M N W G E J E I E E N
G R A A R J U T H M O I S Q U R G E C G
X O E R A F W I B G D S A Q X V Z R V O
Q L Y F G U J H P S I A R B I C M T X R
M A A A E O O W Z N F A L J O Y R S S I
N I H H I X S A G L D A R E K C M L P A
J H S T N O R N B I S J A F Y X T Y G X
U P I E N D Y N V H A N N A H L Y R A D
Y O R R E A X A K J N N I D W L C E U D
O S T A J W D V G D F U D V M F O M D K
```

ALYSSA MILANO	EVA LONGORIA	MERYL STREEP
ARETHA FRANKLIN	GRACE KELLY	SOPHIA LOREN
BETTE DAVIS	JENNIE GARTH	TOM DALEY
DARYL HANNAH	KATHERINE HEIGL	TRISHA YEARWOOD
DAVID ARQUETTE	KATY PERRY	VANNA WHITE
DEBRA MESSING	KURT COBAIN	

 **Word Scramble 1**

Unscramble the words to find words that match the scramble's theme.

KNITTER'S GLOSSARY

RTNTEAP   _ _ _ _ _ _ _

STINA TISTCH   _ _ _ _ _   _ _ _ _ _ _

SATC NO   _ _ _ _   _ _

BNGIE   _ _ _ _ _

NOTFR OLOP   _ _ _ _ _   _ _ _ _

BCEAL EDELEN   _ _ _ _ _   _ _ _ _ _ _

ARNY ROEV   _ _ _ _   _ _ _ _

RGFOGGIN   _ _ _ _ _ _ _ _

TAREPE   _ _ _ _ _ _

ARTEEANTL   _ _ _ _ _ _ _ _ _

RULP   _ _ _ _

GTARRE THSCIT   _ _ _ _ _ _   _ _ _ _ _ _

RAB NAIECSRE   _ _ _   _ _ _ _ _ _ _ _

CNHNELA   _ _ _ _ _ _ _

WOR   _ _ _

WNGRO SDEI   _ _ _ _ _   _ _ _ _

TIRHG EDSI   _ _ _ _ _   _ _ _ _

TUHNOTELOB   _ _ _ _ _ _ _ _ _

IBDN FFO   _ _ _ _   _ _ _

PISL ICTSTH   _ _ _ _   _ _ _ _ _ _

ENNOSTI   _ _ _ _ _ _ _

 Word Scramble 2

Unscramble the words to find words that match the scramble's theme.

KNITTING TERMS

NKSTLOIP _ _ _ _ _ _ _ _

OWLOLF _ _ _ _ _ _

RESCEEDA _ _ _ _ _ _ _ _

RVSEREE _ _ _ _ _ _ _

NETOUICN _ _ _ _ _ _ _ _

CIPK PU _ _ _ _ _ _

TEBNEWE _ _ _ _ _ _ _

CRIEAENS _ _ _ _ _ _ _ _

POLO _ _ _ _

AIBS _ _ _ _

LEEDNE _ _ _ _ _ _

IMAN ROOCL _ _ _ _   _ _ _ _ _

IVENSLIIB MAES _ _ _ _ _ _ _ _ _   _ _ _ _

CTOTSARN CLORO _ _ _ _ _ _ _ _   _ _ _ _ _

RWPA NAD UNTR _ _ _ _   _ _ _   _ _ _ _

PAECL KMARER _ _ _ _ _   _ _ _ _ _ _

OEKTITECTSN SCITHT _ _ _ _ _ _ _ _ _ _   _ _ _ _ _ _

ITEKNSIW _ _ _ _ _ _ _ _

WPRLIESU _ _ _ _ _ _ _ _

KWOR EENV _ _ _ _   _ _ _ _

CSKTACIBHT _ _ _ _ _ _ _ _ _ _

TNBALEK CIHTST _ _ _ _ _ _ _   _ _ _ _ _ _

Criss Cross 1

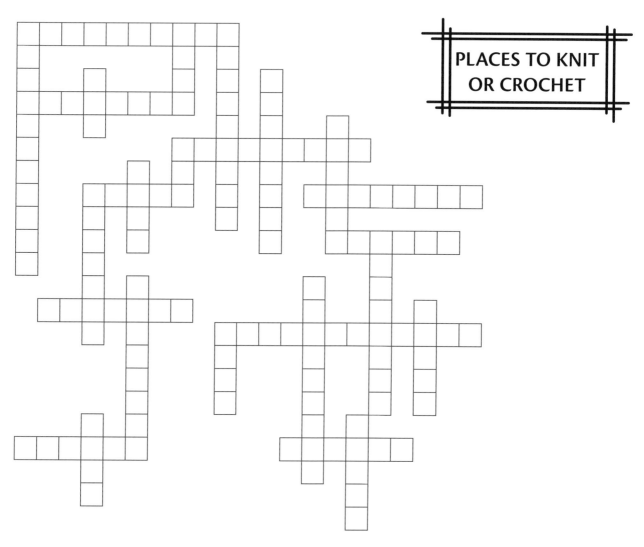

PLACES TO KNIT
OR CROCHET

12 letters

SWIMMING POOL

11 letters

CARPOOL LINE

10 letters

COFFEE SHOP

9 letters

BREAK ROOM

GAME NIGHT

PARK BENCH

8 letters

AIRPLANE

BACKYARD

BALL GAME

FESTIVAL

PLAYDATE

7 letters

CAMPING

CONCERT

6 letters

CHURCH

MOVIES

SCHOOL

SUBWAY

5 letters

CLASS

HOTEL

TRAIN

4 letters

HOME

SHOP

TAXI

WORK

3 letters

BUS

GYM

Criss Cross 2

GUILD MEETING

14 letters
CHARITY PROJECT

12 letters
MEETING PLACE

11 letters
MAKE AND TAKE
MEMBERS ONLY

10 letters
FUNDRAISER

9 letters
COMMUNITY
DOOR PRIZE
FIELD TRIP
YARN CRAWL

8 letters
CALENDAR
OFFICERS
TEACHING
WORKSHOP
YARN SWAP

7 letters
BUS TOUR
CONTEST
LECTURE
LIBRARY
MEMBERS
RETREAT
SHOP HOP

6 letters
CHURCH
SKILLS

5 letters
BOARD
CLASS
GUILD

4 letters
DEMO
DUES
SHOW

🪡 Word RoundUp 1

◀ CRAFT IT CUTE ▶

```
W K Q O W X H J W R E T T O P Y R R A H
E A L L Y O U K N I T I S L O V E P M M
G C A R O S E W F G S K I R I D U K Y G
H B N W L T L F G H U U C E R S W L Z H
O E N G I M O S O X S A Q R H W I E N E
S G I I V S Z L I R D U N E T T Y N I L
T N V T W G I F A M O Z E Z T M P I L L
B I E R C D X W L M P N Y L O U Y M R O
U D R E A I R A F A V S E Q T G S E E K
S D S Y W A V M Z S M P O G V E I B W I
T E A R T A B K Q G O I T N L L A U O T
E W R S K J J H G N A D N C S B T O H T
R C Y U Q F O H Y S N U E G A B N Y S Y
S B I B I R T H D A Y L I V O U E L Y D
Q D U V S G S O Z K C P A S Z B G O B U
J A I O G A R F I E L D T Z J E A O A L
D L O R D O F T H E R I N G S K M W B S
```

☐ ☐ ☐ ☐ ☐ ☐ 6 movie-inspired amigurumi

☐ ☐ ☐ ☐ ☐ 5 occasions to craft a gift

☐ ☐ ☐ ☐ 4 shades of pink

☐ ☐ ☐ 3 famous cats to crochet

☐ ☐ 2 Valentine puns for knitters

Word RoundUp 2

SOPHISTICATED STYLE

```
Z R Y I Z I A U D R E Y H E P B U R N I
C K D L Y O R I G S I F S G N I R R A E
H A J A R S E O S B H N B W G E C A R G
T K P V U W P C D S H A D D G Q Q S Y V
A F D E X E X T N X O Z W I T D B W Z T
B V R K U A Y Z A E R R X L V K R Q O D
L N F U L T H L K Y L Y E N Z K T Z O C
E D K T U E C A A R O U J D R C A I Z H
C M O M D R O V W L N T P B A M L Z D O
L H S R O P O R E J L P A O O I M R V C
O S J H V W R C N Q S U O V E M T J O N
T P H K R U B V Q D C W M S O K H R E U
H D C U F U H Q P O L Y E N Z L K Y O C
D Z M C S H G C H O K E R L A H I B Z P
D H E V A L O N G O R I A P Y G O M Y B
V A N E S S A R E D G R A V E T E Z E F
S O P H I S T I C A T I O N L G S M B D
```

☐ ☐ ☐ ☐ ☐ ☐   6 famous women who knit or crochet

☐ ☐ ☐ ☐ ☐   5 words for elegance

☐ ☐ ☐ ☐   4 shoulder-covering knitwear

☐ ☐ ☐   3 jewelry to crochet

☐ ☐   2 lacework home decor

Logic Puzzle 1

(Easy) **SHOPPING FUN**

Four women went to the local yarn store. They bought different items but each one forgot to buy something. Match the crafters with how much they spent and find out what they each forgot to purchase.

1. Peggy forgot to buy variegated yarn.

2. Becca spent $10 less than the woman that forgot to buy a crochet hook.

3. Jean spent $25.

4. The woman who spent $45 is either Becca or the one who forgot to buy needles.

		SPENT				FORGOT			
		$15	$25	$35	$45	Variegated Yarn	Needles	Crochet Hook	Pattern
SHOPPER	Peggy								
	Suzy								
	Jean								
	Becca								
FORGOT	Variegated Yarn								
	Needles								
	Crochet Hook								
	Pattern								

SHOPPER	SPENT	FORGOT
Peggy		
Suzy		
Jean		
Becca		

Logic Puzzle 2

Easy — **MISSING HOOKS**

Four grandkids helped their Nana look all over the house for her missing crochet hooks. Each child found a hook of a different color and size. Match the name of the grandchild who found each lost crochet hook, naming its size and color.

1. Ronny found the white hook.

2. The size 4 hook that was found is either bamboo or pink.

3. Alice's hook was 4 numbers bigger than Bernie's.

4. Ronny found a hook 4 numbers larger than the bamboo one.

5. Bernie's hook was bronze.

		HOOK SIZE				COLOR			
		4	6	8	10	Bronze	Silver	Bamboo	Pink
NAME	Bernie								
	Alice								
	Ronny								
	Olivia								
COLOR	Bronze								
	Silver								
	Bamboo								
	Pink								

NAME	HOOK SIZE	COLOR
Bernie		
Alice		
Ronny		
Olivia		

Word Mine 1

See how many words you can make out of the letters in popular yarn types!

┌─ YARN TYPES ─┐

PLANT

4-letter words (3)	3-letter words (12)	2-letter words (7)
— — — —	— — —	— —
— — — —	— — —	— —
— — — —	— — —	— —
	— — —	— —
	— — —	— —
	— — —	— —
	— — —	— —
	— — —	
	— — —	
	— — —	
	— — —	
	— — —	

Word Mine 2

See how many words you can make out of the letters in popular yarn types!

┌─ YARN TYPES ─┐

COTTON

└──────────────┘

5-letter word (1)

— — — — —

4-letter words (7)

— — — —

— — — —

— — — —

— — — —

— — — —

— — — —

— — — —

3-letter words (10)

— — —

— — —

— — —

— — —

— — —

— — —

— — —

— — —

— — —

2-letter words (3)

— —

— —

— —

Crossword Puzzle 2

KNIT-TERMINOLOGY

ACROSS

4 stitch to knit when you're watching a movie

5 step and a hop

6 band of frequencies used in television transmission

9 do again

10 knitting needles measured in these

14 find one in a haystack?

16 to propel with oars

19 rip-it, rip-it

21 prep needle for knitting (2 wds)

22 "We Go _____," from Grease

23 remove stitches from needles (2 wds)

24 work knit stitches backwards to find a mistake

25 the opposite of 3 Down

DOWN

1 add stitches to the needle that were previously bound off (2 wds)

2 to knit with no increase or decrease (2 wds)

3 get more stitches in a row

5 step on a banana peel?

7 start here

8 back side of a knit stitch

11 stitches left on the needle

12 rock and hard place

13 foreground coil (2 wds)

15 YO, for short (2 wds)

17 one of prevention is worth a pound of cure

18 resume

20 common snake or type of stitch

Crossword Puzzle 3

CROCHET, YOU SAY?

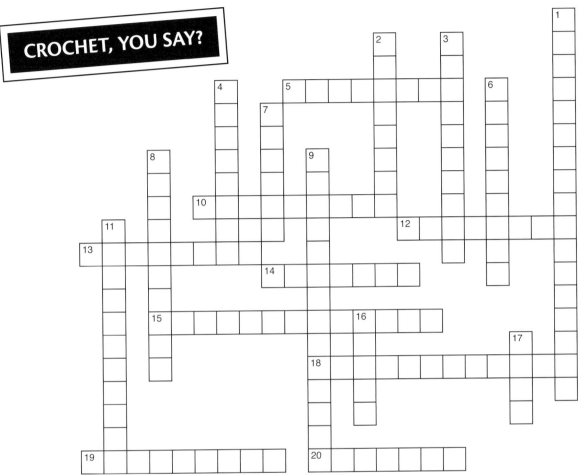

ACROSS

5 V-shaped part of the stitch (2 wds)

10 stitches worked into slip knot (2 wds)

12 work two stitches in the same stitch

13 red rover, red rover, wrap the yarn around the hook once (2 wds)

14 cut it with a knife?

15 a single in the U.K. (2 wds)

18 geriatric geometry (2 wds)

19 the oft forgotten loop underneath (2 wds)

20 sewing crochet pieces together

DOWN

1 almost (not quite) a double crochet (3 wds)

2 helping a project relax and lie flat

3 good stitch for a produce bag (2 wds)

4 combine two stitches into one

6 comfy spot to hold your hook (2 wds)

7 studious way to hold your hook

8 tool used to weave in ends (2 wds)

9 WIP (3 wds)

11 desert animal, or worked in the third loop (2 wds)

16 start each row with this

17 cut it 8 to 10 inches

MEASUREMENTS

```
W L A R G E P P U U Z W B S J B U S T E
G P I N Z M A O K W N Q A J R I J O P M
B A F V B L O N S S P I H I J A R J I I
U N R Z T O V E E I E V N F S I K L O C
H Y U M U R K A N G T E Y X G T L O I B
A L J C E D Z C F Q A I W U M I V R O L
Z S I H R N Z E E J S T V C M J C H I H
R N C A C M T E R H R Q I E L U X U J Z
V E Y F U L U U O O C E T V M J E U G H
N A J I T I J E V H E E T F E G P R U P
V N D T K N S S B O R A E E U R E T E M
J E K S P I Q Q O Q C R S A M L L A M S
M Q N R Z D E Z J U E X G E U I O V R P
Q I E E L S K X S N N R I R M Q T X W M
V I T O O T H I C Z A C Y S H H C N I B
U T K O L J F E N M A A E Q O F M E E C
X Q L S O V E R S I Z E D U Y G O E M C
```

BUST	INCH	OUNCE
CENTIMETER	LARGE	OVERSIZED
CIRCUMFERENCE	LOOSE	POSITIVE
GARMENT	MEDIUM	SMALL
GAUGE	METER	SHOE SIZE
GRAM	MILLIMETER	YARD
HIPS	RULER	ZERO EASE
HOOK	NEGATIVE	WAIST

Word Search 4

YARN BRANDS

```
B X G I C E Y A R N S D N A R B N O I L
R Q V T A H K I O H Z D Q T I I B B O H
I B I S P A S Q V I A S S O R G A N A L
R B X I O S D Z X P Q J U D W Q W N A C
E Y E U D Z A J I C S N R A Y S U T O L
I E V F E K E X J A W O L U S N O T A P
M O S W E G R U O R W B L Y R K A D A R
E J L K W D H L O O W Y X E S Y Z A R C
R X O N T S T O W N D Z R A T I L J C T
P L V I N H D O E H Y R Q Z D F A F A R
Y Z E T Y T N W B E R N A T K R A L S A
S R S P L U A Y N V U G Z S E E T Y C E
H B E I K O S Z Y B C C Y V S N H H A H
D X S C O M P O E G B D A R H A A Y D D
T R O K O Y O C B S N D D Y K N L W E E
S V E S R L O Q P E O E O Z R S E P O R
R F U Z B P L D W M A R P U P P Y H W R
```

BERNAT	ICE YARNS	PLASSARD
BROOKLYN TWEED	KNIT PICKS	PLYMOUTH
CARON	LANA GROSSA	PREMIER
CASCADE	LION BRAND	PUPPY
CLOURMART	LOOPS AND THREADS	RED HEART
COZY WOOL	LOTUS YARNS	ROWAN
CRAZY SEXY WOOL	MODA VERA	TAHKI
HOBBII	PATONS	WENDY

 Word Scramble 3

Unscramble the words to find words that match the scramble's theme.

CRAFT EVERYWHERE

WBYSAU _ _ _ _ _ _

YETPLAAD _ _ _ _ _ _ _

AEMG HNITG _ _ _ _ _ _ _ _ _

SLOOCH _ _ _ _ _ _

OSEVMI _ _ _ _ _ _

RLOCPAO EINL _ _ _ _ _ _ _ _ _ _ _

HCUHCR _ _ _ _ _ _

LABL MAGE _ _ _ _ _ _ _ _

KRAP CHNBE _ _ _ _ _ _ _ _ _

IRTNA _ _ _ _ _

OHLET _ _ _ _ _

GACPNMI _ _ _ _ _ _ _

AEKRB OROM _ _ _ _ _ _ _ _ _ _

OEHM _ _ _ _

RTATREE _ _ _ _ _ _ _

AIXT _ _ _ _

OATVICAN _ _ _ _ _ _ _ _

IGNWMSIM LOPO _ _ _ _ _ _ _ _ _ _ _ _

EEFCOF OHSP _ _ _ _ _ _ _ _ _ _

RCAABYKD _ _ _ _ _ _ _ _

IAROTPR _ _ _ _ _ _ _

Word Scramble 4

Unscramble the words to find words that match the scramble's theme.

CROCHET TERMS 1

GAMESNI _ _ _ _ _ _ _

BICLGNKO _ _ _ _ _ _ _ _

OHOK _ _ _ _

SPOT _ _ _ _

IRPPWANG _ _ _ _ _ _ _ _

SCENIERA _ _ _ _ _ _ _ _

TFENAS
FOF _ _ _ _ _ _   _ _ _

GFNAHA _ _ _ _ _ _

TSLSEA _ _ _ _ _ _

RUNT _ _ _ _

IADRB _ _ _ _ _

IET FOF _ _ _   _ _ _

SIPL
TNKO _ _ _ _   _ _ _ _

DPRAETE OHKO _ _ _ _ _ _ _   _ _ _ _

SHME HITCST _ _ _ _   _ _ _ _ _ _

TIPCO CTTISH _ _ _ _ _   _ _ _ _ _ _

RYNANG QEASRU _ _ _ _ _ _   _ _ _ _ _ _

NNIILE OKOH _ _ _ _ _ _   _ _ _ _ _

RPPOCNO TSHTIC _ _ _ _ _ _ _   _ _ _ _ _ _

IGRNKWO RYNA _ _ _ _ _ _ _   _ _ _ _ _

NIEGFR CHETORC _ _ _ _ _ _   _ _ _ _ _ _ _

NIOJNIG AESQSUR _ _ _ _ _ _   _ _ _ _ _ _ _

LFAH EUBDLO
HRCTOCE _ _ _ _   _ _ _ _ _ _   _ _ _ _ _ _ _

ERYBR CTTHSI _ _ _ _ _   _ _ _ _ _ _

AKBC SPLOO _ _ _ _   _ _ _ _ _

TINGRNU IACNH _ _ _ _ _ _ _   _ _ _ _ _

Criss Cross 3

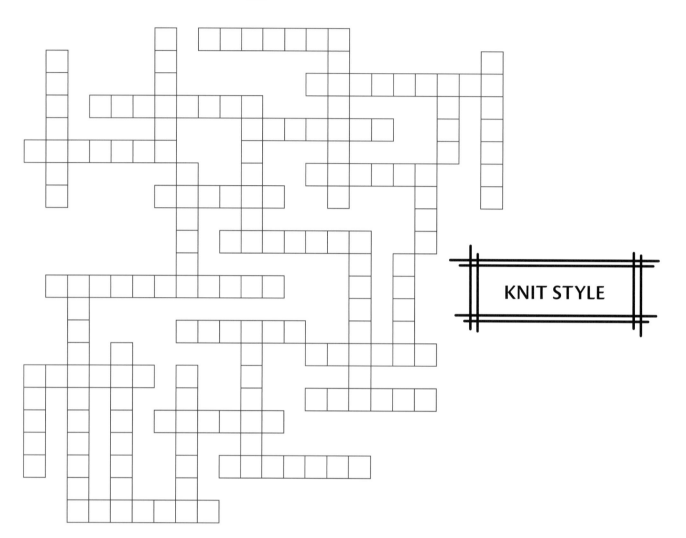

KNIT STYLE

11 letters

ACCESSORIES

FASHIONABLE

9 letters

BEAUTIFUL

8 letters

CHEERFUL

CLOTHING

HANDMADE

WARDROBE

7 letters

APPAREL

CLASSIC

FASHION

GARMENT

HIPSTER

ORGANIC

STYLISH

SWEATER

TEXTILE

TEXTURE

VINTAGE

6 letters

AUTUMN

CASUAL

COTTON

JUMPER

PRETTY

RUSTIC

SEASON

UNIQUE

WINTER

5 letters

COMFY

RETRO

4 letters

COZY

FALL

Criss Cross 4

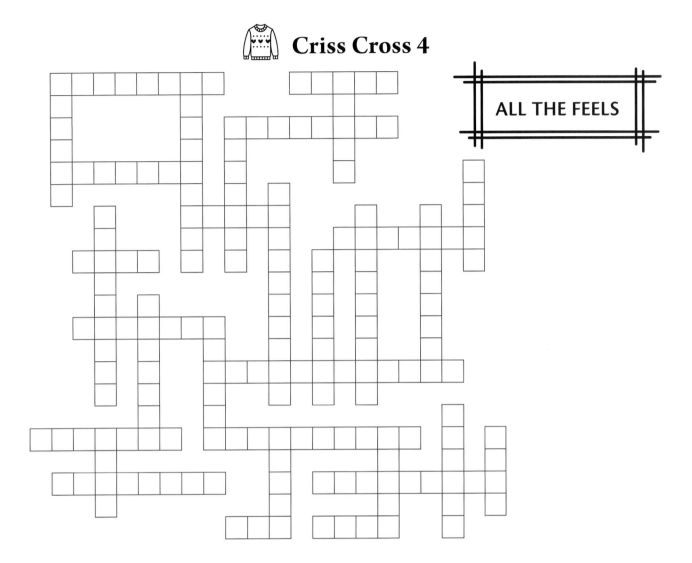

ALL THE FEELS

12 letters

STRESS-RELIEF

10 letters

ENTHUSIASM

FRUSTRATED

9 letters

ENJOYMENT

FULFILLED

SATISFIED

WELL-BEING

8 letters

ADDICTED

CONFUSED

DEVOTION

PLEASURE

7 letters

DELIGHT

ECSTASY

HARMONY

PASSION

PUZZLED

RELAXED

SUCCESS

6 letters

AMUSED

DESIRE

MAKING

5 letters

BLISS

EAGER

HAPPY

HOBBY

PRIDE

SMILE

4 letters

BODY

GLEE

LOVE

MIND

3 letters

JOY

Word RoundUp 3

YARN KNOWLEDGE

```
U L H C N I S R L O D K E R E M H S A C
V O B A N Z E A E E O O R J O O B M A B
S C E I N C V M I D E C F R M T A Z F W
S A R V A G O A Z F H U O E N I L N O M
V L N X C P O Q P J G E F T D N P L I Y
U Y A T M I G R K R S I A J T R E T E M
J A T O V P L Y A J E A G R G O H Q R W
D R P S T A Z Y Q C V T X L T H N F T I
N N J C B T H J R F I O E Q W A L E D D
A S K V B O K L J C H O L M L Q G N A C
R H K W O N D J E S A K N H I W O O O V
B O G A B S S Z T S T I N D K T Y W G E
N P I N B F B T W F S R L A R Q N O N F
O A Q L L P Q O R G M A L M W A L E S O
I A X N E K O N R G N N T C Y O Y G C B
L H U U E L C H A P C Z C D J B R U I O
```

☐ ☐ ☐ ☐ ☐ ☐ 6 yarn fiber types

☐ ☐ ☐ ☐ ☐ 5 yarn name brands

☐ ☐ ☐ ☐ 4 measurements for length

☐ ☐ ☐ 3 embellishments from yarn

☐ ☐ 2 places to buy yarn

Word RoundUp 4

CROCHET TO KNOW

```
F A D P L H E A D B A N D E C J P K Y U
R F R T V S G C Y M N A I R A V A B L
E I E V V J S B Y R P G B J L F Z U W W
T M S P B G C Z T H O F G R U A O Y B I
A A S T C M O G O I H C G T M U E Q Z I
E K O B Y C N N T T K G H U A U E S I I
W K E A P E E P B I H M D E L E S D N G
S E R U I C R B X C V Q E M T Y P C E U
C L C Q A G T U N I S I A N K H R E V Y
A D R S C D X G S E N S E P Q E O B R P
R E E N F F C W Q A R E L S A M U O A E
F E V A U U R F X O E S R S A S U T K C
G N O I L K T T S P E M E N T E T E H H
S N N N R W J S W T L H E C C E R A E V
I R R S R X I U N U B Q B P R P I C D C
F A A O M C Z C D O F W U N A N K R E R
Z Y Y B S D N E N I E V A E W T T N S D
```

☐ ☐ ☐ ☐ ☐ ☐ 6 pattern terms

☐ ☐ ☐ ☐ ☐ 5 tools

☐ ☐ ☐ ☐ 4 beginner projects

☐ ☐ ☐ 3 world crochet styles

☐ ☐ 2 challenging projects

🧦 Logic Puzzle 3

Four sisters each started knitting a project in January, but they all finished at different times. Use the clues to find out how many skeins they used and in what month they finished their projects.

1. The sister who finished her project in February used more skeins than Sonia.

2. Rhonda used 3 skeins.

3. Sonia finished her project in April.

4. Eileen used 1 skein less than the knitter who finished in June.

		SKEINS				MONTH			
		3	4	5	6	February	April	June	September
NAME	Eileen								
	Fay								
	Sonia								
	Rhonda								
MONTH	February								
	April								
	June								
	September								

NAME	SKEINS	MONTH
Eileen		
Fay		
Sonia		
Rhonda		

Logic Puzzle 4

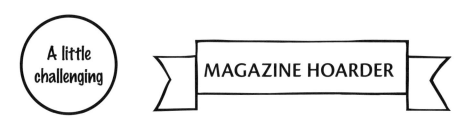

A little challenging

MAGAZINE HOARDER

Annette collects knitting magazines from different countries. Each has a different number of patterns. Find out how much the international knitting magazines cost and how many patterns each has inside.

1. The British magazine has 10 patterns.

2. The magazine with 8 patterns is either Australian or it costs $4.50.

3. The Canadian magazine has fewer patterns than the Icelandic one.

4. The magazine that charged $8.50 has 4 fewer patterns than the British one.

5. The magazine that costs $7 has 2 more patterns than the Icelandic magazine.

		PATTERN COUNT				PRICE			
		4	6	8	10	$5.50	$7	$8.50	$10
NATIONALITY	Canadian								
	British								
	Icelandic								
	Australian								
PRICE	$5.50								
	$7								
	$8.50								
	$10								

NATIONALITY	PATTERN COUNT	PRICE
Canadian		
British		
Icelandic		
Australian		

Word Mine 3

See how many words you can make out of the letters in popular yarn types!

┌─── YARN TYPES ───┐

R A Y O N

└──────────────────┘

4-letter words (3)	3-letter words (10)	2-letter words (10)
— — — —	— — —	— —
— — — —	— — —	— —
— — — —	— — —	— —
	— — —	— —
	— — —	— —
	— — —	— —
	— — —	— —
	— — —	— —
	— — —	— —
	— — —	— —

Word Mine 4

See how many words you can make out of the letters in popular yarn types!

┌─── YARN TYPES ───┐
BAMBOO
└──────────────────┘

5-letter word (1)

— — — — —

4-letter words (5)

— — — —

— — — —

— — — —

— — — —

— — — —

3-letter words (9)

— — —

— — —

— — —

— — —

— — —

— — —

— — —

— — —

— — —

2-letter words (7)

— —

— —

— —

— —

— —

— —

— —

Crossword Puzzle 4

TOOLS OF THE TRADE

ACROSS

4 Vogue Knitting, for one

5 crochet hook with cone-like throat

8 foam board used to shape yarn projects (2 wds)

12 vessel that keeps yarn untangled while you work (2 wds)

13 tiny but useful tools to keep your knitting on track (2 wds)

14 maker's mark on finished item

15 type of needle used to knit in the round for small items (2 wds)

20 flat tool for measuring rows and stitches (2 wds)

21 pattern compendium for the coffee table

22 tiny tools used for blocking knitting or crochet

23 crochet hook with a notch cut at the throat

24 point protectors

DOWN

1 tool used for a fisherman's sweater (2 wds)

2 ideal needles for knitting in the round

3 spritzer for wet blocking (2 wds)

6 fabric wrap for taking needles on the go (2 wds)

7 2016 documentary about fiber arts in culture

9 body size finder (2 wds)

10 *Peter Pan* antagonist

11 snip snip

16 takes yarn from hank to usable form quickly

17 crafting instructions

18 useful to keep yarn colors contained during colorwork

19 cowhide for bag handles

Crossword Puzzle 5

KNIT-TERTAINMENT

ACROSS

1   Apple Music competitor

4   *Survivor* started it (2 wds)

7   The Parenthood, for one

8   Jim Carrey's specialty

9   Hawkins, Ind. sci-fi (2 wds)

13   IG, for short

16   hands-free novel

19   video tutorials hub

20   Joe Exotic's smash hit (2 wds)

21   Hell's Kitchen is one (2 wds)

DOWN

2   Central Perk

3   head to NPR to catch one

5   Pam Beesly's workplace (2 wds)

6   RIP, McDreamy (2 wds)

7   Crawley family drama (2 wds)

10   Stephen King genre

11   Mulder & Scully (3 wds)

12   Michael Moore genre

14   Thank you for being a friend (2 wds)

15   romantic comedy, i.e. (2 wds)

17   Handmaid's Tale home

18   ____ and chill

Word Search 5

EXOTIC PLACES TO KNIT

```
A F K Z Z M S R K P I H S E S I U R C A
Q A H R M N G K H M A K Z C L I V Y L F
X L U I K V E W B M H F L I G W P L T W
R O K S A R K W M G Y O Y A K C I Y H F
B N V T T H A O Z M L T T S W N G D C F
A D Y T A R C P N E I N P T C D X Y A H
H O O R F K A A L C A A C L U S R Q Y T
A N I I A Z E L K A D L U H E B V A D M
M R J Y F B C R I N N S A R W M J E O H
A I Q F B C O H A A I O I N A H C A E B
S Z K I R Y A L A V L A I R D L T L U D
G Z R L W V E P E I S G O T D W Q Z T W
H A B E A R Z R E O S B M I A N L O O P
C N N L I L E J N C A E O S O N A V L G
L V L B T S W E J R O B N I O O I L R Z
Y I E E O W U Z O P E D U H U J Q J S C
V E Q R M B R B S E V I D L A M J R F I
```

ALL INCLUSIVE RESORT	CAPE COD	ISLAND
AUSTRALIA	CHAISE	MALDIVES
BAHAMAS	CRUISE SHIP	NATIONAL PARK
BEACH	FIJI	NEW YORK CITY
BOARDWALK	HAMMOCK	NEW ZEALAND
BORA BORA	HOT TUB	POOL
BUENOS AIRES	LONDON	SPA
CARIBBEAN	IRELAND	VILLA
		YACHT

Word Search 6

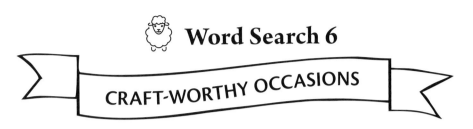

CRAFT-WORTHY OCCASIONS

```
U P R Z A H A Y C X N O I T A U D A R G
Q F E T P N A S B H S A M T S I R H C B
M H B N N V N N B I G N I D D E W Z O B
U I O V C E F I U A R D I E H T W B N A
Q W M A W O M A V K B T X S R W D N G C
Q B D L D N U E T E K Y H N X R H O R K
E A M E F O M R R H R A S D G V H I A T
S P L N N L P G A I E S H H A R W T T O
U T B T E T T T O G T R A N O Y Z O U S
A I E I E F F E I Z E E S R D W I M L C
C S S N W A Y M P O K M R D Y R E O A H
E M L E O A D I P W N E E J A P N R T O
B C N S L Z O A T H E P U N Q Y S P I O
T F P D L N W Q V Y A N R F T F G B O L
S Z K A A A W H O L I D A Y X B F L N M
U L B Y H W K F X F S Y M P A T H Y S F
J A G R G K U M O Y Y A D S R E H T O M
```

ADOPTION	ENCOURAGEMENT	PROMOTION
ANNIVERSARY	FATHER'S DAY	NEW PET
BABY SHOWER	GRADUATION	MOTHER'S DAY
BACK TO SCHOOL	HALLOWEEN	RETIREMENT
BAPTISM	HANUKKAH	SYMPATHY
BIRTHDAY	HOLIDAY	VALENTINE'S DAY
CHRISTMAS	JUST BECAUSE	WEDDING
CONGRATULATIONS	KWANZAA	

Word Scramble 5

Unscramble the words to find words that match the scramble's theme.

CROCHET TERMS 2

HITPCSWHTI
AMES _ _ _ _ _ _ _ _ _ _ _ _ _ _

GCIMA IRGN _ _ _ _ _ _ _ _ _ _

PORD HICTTS _ _ _ _ _ _ _ _ _ _

NI HET OUNDR _ _ _ _ _ _ _ _ _ _

HLLES THITSC _ _ _ _ _ _ _ _ _ _ _ _

CTTIHS
AKERRM _ _ _ _ _ _ _ _ _ _ _ _ _

UEAGG _ _ _ _ _

RANY ROEV _ _ _ _ _ _ _ _

NHACI _ _ _ _ _

UOLBED
ORCCEHT _ _ _ _ _ _ _ _ _ _ _ _ _

AELCM TCHTIS _ _ _ _ _ _ _ _ _ _ _

NIIUNTAS
CRHECTO _ _ _ _ _ _ _ _ _ _ _ _ _ _ _

LSEIGN
COHCTER _ _ _ _ _ _ _ _ _ _ _ _ _

HBMUT TSER _ _ _ _ _ _ _ _ _ _

LPIS TTIHCS _ _ _ _ _ _ _ _ _ _

ALTI _ _ _ _

POT OSPOL _ _ _ _ _ _ _ _

PELITR
ROCETCH _ _ _ _ _ _ _ _ _ _ _ _ _

IHTDR LPOO _ _ _ _ _ _ _ _ _ _

INSNETO _ _ _ _ _ _ _

YNAR NLDEEE _ _ _ _ _ _ _ _ _ _ _

RCEDEASE _ _ _ _ _ _ _ _

AWEEV
IN DSNE _ _ _ _ _ _ _ _ _ _ _ _

Word Scramble 6

Unscramble the words to find words that match the scramble's theme.

TYPES OF YARN

PHME _ _ _ _

ANRA _ _ _ _

CUYNKH _ _ _ _ _ _

NNIEL _ _ _ _ _ _ _

ATERIVEAGD _ _ _ _ _ _ _ _ _

CAPAALA _ _ _ _ _ _ _

EHRPSUSW
OWLO _ _ _ _ _ _ _ _ _ _ _

RICLAYC _ _ _ _ _ _ _

NARLP _ _ _ _ _

DOEWTSR _ _ _ _ _ _ _

RAOHIM _ _ _ _ _ _

LOWO _ _ _ _

CNOOTT _ _ _ _ _ _

OPTRS _ _ _ _ _

ROENIM _ _ _ _ _ _

RGNOAA _ _ _ _ _ _

ENYCSHTTI _ _ _ _ _ _ _ _ _

PNHSUOME _ _ _ _ _ _ _ _

IKSL _ _ _ _

OBMOBA _ _ _ _ _ _

GIRVNO _ _ _ _ _ _

RUNTAAL _ _ _ _ _ _ _

GEAVN _ _ _ _ _

CEERMSAH _ _ _ _ _ _ _ _

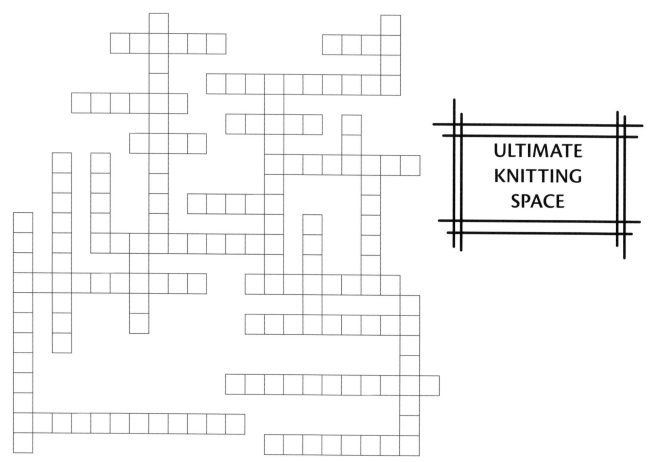

Criss Cross 5

ULTIMATE
KNITTING
SPACE

12 letters

FRESH FLOWERS

PERSONAL CHEF

RECORD PLAYER

11 letters

CHARCUTERIE

FAVORITE PET

10 letters

COMFY CHAIR

SCENIC VIEW

PORCH SWING

TAKE IT EASY

9 letters

FIREPLACE

8 letters

COLORFUL

COZY NOOK

PEACEFUL

RELAXING

7 letters

OTTOMAN

6 letters

CREATE

DREAMY

TEAPOT

5 letters

CRAFT

MOVIE

MUSIC

QUIET

4 letters

CALM

SNUG

YARN

3 letters

ZEN

Criss Cross 6

CROCHET ALL DAY

13 letters

FINGER CROCHET

12 letters

STITCH MARKER

11 letters

TAPERED HOOK

WEAVE IN ENDS

10 letters

INLINE HOOK

MESH STITCH

SLIP STITCH

YARN NEEDLE

9 letters

MAGIC RING

THIRD LOOP

THUMB REST

8 letters

BLOCKING

SLIP KNOT

TOP LOOPS

YARN OVER

7 letters

SEAMING

TENSION

6 letters

DOUBLE

SINGLE

TIE OFF

TRIPLE

5 letters

CHAIN

GAUGE

4 letters

POST

TAIL

TURN

3 letters

WIP

Word RoundUp 5

KNIT KNOW-HOW

```
J  J  M  Y  T  B  G  S  R  E  K  R  A  M  H  C  T  I  T  S
B  W  P  X  Z  O  U  Q  L  I  D  D  Q  Z  M  M  E  J  A  G
I  U  Q  U  Z  E  Y  X  T  I  T  O  B  A  B  A  D  N  P  I
W  L  L  C  W  F  O  C  F  Y  X  X  O  I  X  T  F  M  U  M
Q  S  U  K  L  Q  H  Z  R  I  R  X  N  U  G  B  Y  S  K  R
R  T  O  J  Y  E  C  R  O  J  N  D  N  I  W  V  M  P  C  F
Y  O  K  K  N  Y  E  M  F  E  O  G  E  W  C  L  H  U  I  H
F  C  W  E  O  T  X  P  T  F  L  R  E  A  F  Q  K  R  P  Z
R  K  R  C  R  Q  L  E  F  V  U  D  S  R  W  C  D  L  C  Z
I  I  M  A  O  R  T  W  Z  S  F  T  E  U  I  Y  S  T  E  K
A  N  G  C  S  U  Y  B  A  F  O  W  T  E  B  N  X  N  J  L
F  E  R  J  A  L  N  E  O  N  P  R  X  S  N  M  G  U  N  V
T  T  L  C  D  O  M  T  D  E  T  S  R  O  W  E  K  V  E  C
F  T  X  R  D  E  N  E  E  J  E  O  K  N  I  T  L  P  P  O
A  E  B  S  P  O  R  T  H  R  U  B  C  Z  X  M  O  B  G  C
R  T  J  A  G  V  E  I  X  M  R  E  D  N  I  W  L  L  A  B
C  H  T  W  O  R  K  E  V  E  N  P  E  S  Q  K  T  M  K  C
```

☐ ☐ ☐ ☐ ☐ ☐   6 actions in knitting

☐ ☐ ☐ ☐ ☐   5 notions

☐ ☐ ☐ ☐   4 yarn weights

☐ ☐ ☐   3 knit stitches

☐ ☐   2 places to sell knits

Word RoundUp 6

WISH LIST

```
X V D A O I N E D I R P S R E T T I N K
M Q I C L O V E R R C W L B D S Y M S S
H C M C J F P D N Q S G Z T K K I C T V
E H N Y U G P Y G I A S N J D Q I I U N
A I R B A N T B B R H S P D F S T B N S
F A F B O O A L U D K W V B S C I H D G
T O I O G Y I P A C E N H O H P B I U H
E G P S U F E R I B U F R H D W C A V D
R O S I P K J P S X E S O Y F P N Q I P
N O A L G O T Z I H V L E E L A I F C Q
O U O K A I B G S A D R S G C N M R Z S
O E C N N U N X O E E A J O N U X Y Q B
N I N K A I R T R M C L H O T I E C R X
A H A P N A J S H K W S R P J D N R Q P
F R S E Q Y T S O A T R X D Z E D R X A
I J V D F H A O V S L E A H C I M Q O S
A E W P C C H S W A T C H R U L E R W M
```

☐ ☐ ☐ ☐ ☐ ☐ 6 needle brands

☐ ☐ ☐ ☐ ☐ 5 crochet notions

☐ ☐ ☐ ☐ 4 luxury yarns

☐ ☐ ☐ 3 times to knit

☐ ☐ 2 big box craft stores

🧦 Logic Puzzle 5

A little challenging

PDF PATTERNS

A knitting megasite wants to recognize some of its most-downloaded PDF patterns released in the last year. Match the name of the pattern with its designer, the number of downloads, and the month it launched.

1. Neither the pattern released in March nor Baby Bunny was designed by Crafty Chic.

2. The pattern launched by Cat Lady Knits was released 2 months later than the one with 3.1 millions downloads.

3. The pattern that took off in June doesn't have 6.8 million downloads.

4. The PDF pattern with 4.2 million downloads launched later than the one from Crafty Chic.

5. Of Arm-Knit Pouf and the pattern launched in May, one has 4.2 million downloads and the other was designed by Patty Purl.

6. The pattern with 3.1 million downloads launched 2 months before the 1-Hour Scarf.

7. Neither the PDF pattern with 4.2 million downloads nor Crochet Cowl is the one designed by Amazing Art.

		PATTERN				DESIGNER				DOWNLOADS			
		Crochet Cowl	Arm-Knit Pouf	Baby Bunny	1-Hour Scarf	Patty Purl	Crafty Chic	Amazing Art	Cat Lady Knits	1.5 million	3.1 million	4.2 million	6.8 million
MONTH	March												
	April												
	May												
	June												
DOWNLOADS	1.5 million												
	3.1 million												
	4.2 million												
	6.8 million												
DESIGNER	Patty Purl												
	Crafty Chic												
	Amazing Art												
	Cat Lady Knits												

MONTH	PATTERN	DESIGNER	DOWNLOADS
March			
April			
May			
June			

Logic Puzzle 6

TV TIME

A few crafters binge-watched popular shows while knitting. Find out what day each of the knitters watched their favorite show and how many episodes they viewed.

1. Either Alex or Paola had their TV marathon on Sunday.

2. Neither Mindy nor Alex watched television on Tuesday.

3. Karen watched exactly 2 episodes.

4. Paola enjoyed more episodes of her favorite show than the knitter who watched *This Is Us*.

5. One more episode of *Game of Thrones* was watched than Alex's choice.

6. Out of Alex and the knitter who watched TV on Tuesday, one enjoyed *Handmaid's Tale* and the other saw 3 episodes.

7. The knitter who watched *This Is Us* saw one more episode than the knitter who crafted on Friday.

		KNITTER				SHOW				DAY			
		Karen	Mindy	Alex	Paola	Game of Thrones	Handmaid's Tale	This Is Us	Gilmore Girls	Saturday	Sunday	Tuesday	Friday
EPISODES	2												
	3												
	4												
	5												
DAY	Saturday												
	Sunday												
	Tuesday												
	Friday												
SHOW	Game of Thrones												
	Handmaid's Tale												
	This Is Us												
	Gilmore Girls												

EPISODES	KNITTER	SHOW	DAY
2			
3			
4			
5			

♡ **Word Mine 5**

See how many words you can make out of the letters in popular yarn types!

┌─ YARN TYPES ─┐

ACRYLIC

6-letter word (1)	5-letter words (5)	4-letter words (15)	3-letter words (15)	2-letter words (7)
— — — — — —	— — — — —	— — — —	— — —	— —
	— — — — —	— — — —	— — —	— —
	— — — — —	— — — —	— — —	— —
	— — — — —	— — — —	— — —	— —
	— — — — —	— — — —	— — —	— —
		— — — —	— — —	— —
		— — — —	— — —	— —
		— — — —	— — —	
		— — — —	— — —	
		— — — —	— — —	
		— — — —	— — —	
		— — — —	— — —	
		— — — —	— — —	
		— — — —	— — —	
		— — — —	— — —	

Word Mine 6

See how many words you can make out of the letters in popular yarn types!

┌─ YARN TYPES ─┐

ANIMAL

6-letter words (2)	5-letter words (8)	4-letter words (16)	3-letter words (16)	2-letter words (11)
_ _ _ _ _ _	_ _ _ _ _	_ _ _ _	_ _ _	_ _
_ _ _ _ _ _	_ _ _ _ _	_ _ _ _	_ _ _	_ _
	_ _ _ _ _	_ _ _ _	_ _ _	_ _
	_ _ _ _ _	_ _ _ _	_ _ _	_ _
	_ _ _ _ _	_ _ _ _	_ _ _	_ _
	_ _ _ _ _	_ _ _ _	_ _ _	_ _
	_ _ _ _ _	_ _ _ _	_ _ _	_ _
	_ _ _ _ _	_ _ _ _	_ _ _	_ _
		_ _ _ _	_ _ _	_ _
		_ _ _ _	_ _ _	_ _
		_ _ _ _	_ _ _	_ _
		_ _ _ _	_ _ _	
		_ _ _ _	_ _ _	
		_ _ _ _	_ _ _	
		_ _ _ _	_ _ _	
		_ _ _ _	_ _ _	

Crossword Puzzle 6

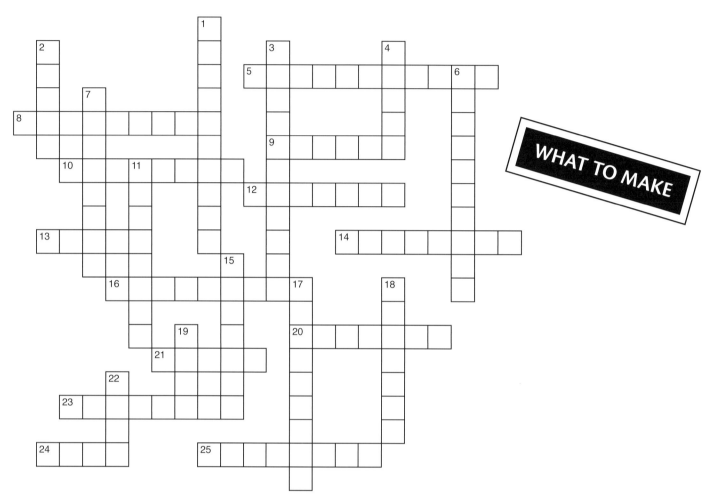

WHAT TO MAKE

ACROSS

5 centerpiece for dining (2 wds)

8 Put your feet up (2 wds)

9 can be slouched or tight on the head

10 Often in a set of 4 or 6

12 Keeps mashed peas at bay (2 wds)

13 beginner's knitting project

14 Dorothy had a red pair

16 square for scrubbing

20 coffee lover gift (2 wds)

21 made in pairs to wear down there

23 wrist dangle

24 handled carrier

25 head cover for medical hair loss (2 wds)

DOWN

1 reusable mop add-on (2 wds)

2 delicate lace decor

3 swaddling tool (2 wds)

4 place to stash your keys

6 sound catcher covers (2 wds)

7 sled or hat

11 filled with fluff

15 afghan

17 term for interior art (2 wds)

18 baby footwear

19 neck warmer

22 cloak

Crossword Puzzle 7

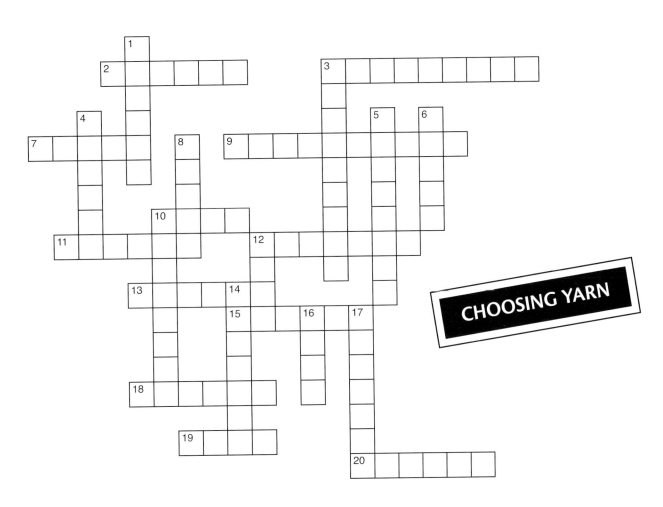

CHOOSING YARN

ACROSS

2 lustrous fiber from the Angora goat

3 not natural

7 upcycled yarn from grocery bags

9 changes color as you go

10 sisal

11 common fiber in modern textiles

12 most popular yarn weight

13 less itchy wool

15 spits like its relatives

18 rabbit wool

19 fiber made by insects

20 bulky, as in yarn

DOWN

1 yarn that's not completely twisted or plied

3 run this wool through the wash

4 panda snack

5 soft yarn, from the "greatest of all time"

6 no animals used

8 from fibers of flax

10 crinkle-look yarn from Lion Brand

12 from sheep fleece

14 _____ Born Killers

16 U.K.'s common yarn weight, thicker than worsted

17 synthetic yarn made from acryonile

Word Search 7

GET SOCIAL

```
O E S V L I N C A U G E B U T U O Y T U
C N T E E K P J M X D P F L S S J K W K
R G U I L D M E E T I N G Y R A R B I L
O Y P F M A R G A T S N I G V E J I T R
C V O R R T G L O M I Y W R I U N Z T E
H R H I R Q I N I Y D J I S D U V J E T
E Y S E J L D K I U P D D A E K J R R F
T T E N C U R B T B P A E G O K R E T A
C D E D S R G E Y O M Q N H L K K D U R
L R F S K H E T T N K O D H C X D I C
U E F F Y O I A T R L X B Y E C B I C S
B B O A L N O S T A E Z J N R M T T T B
H I C C U I A B T I J A X N R L I I E A
M F X M V C C I E H V W T K Y A E C W M
X F M E D L N K E C B E I R W X Y V W T
P O R O M K W C R R A Z P O H S N R A Y
C P P J U T G L B N L F C P H Q R Z E R
```

COFFEE SHOP
COMMUNITY
CRAFTER
CREATIVE
CROCHET CLUB
FACEBOOK
FIBER
FLICKR
FRIENDS

GUILD MEETING
INSTAGRAM
KNIT ALONG
LIBRARY
PANDEMIC
PODCAST
RAVELRY
REDDIT
RETREAT

TIKTOK
TWITCH
TWITTER
VIDEO
YARN BOMBING
YARN SHOP
YOUTUBE

Word Search 8

GROUP GETAWAYS & RETREATS

```
D J P X F M B D Q G I L U R M H S A T S
O Q J S E L F I E S Q Z O Z K U G M B O
O U S E I M O O R W G A J O G D T U V S
R L H S S U A Q X S D Z Q N N V N E N B
P T T K S L B Z A T Q I V L V K R A Y F
R H E V D H K H R Y A R N X B N C J R M
I A O A Z A O I K H I G P E I K G I D E
Z G V T C T P W A D P H D G S R E A U W
E N G Y E H K P A I M S H V O N Y C E M
Z I D L B L E Z W N D T P N D T J M P K
A T D Y I Q A R L L D K I S O E U X F N
V T B W X U J M E I H T E N A L P R I A
S I S F U N P D N E K E E W V U Y D S N
B N P S Y Z L G J G B I M L O W D E L I
T K Z V A I W L E S S O N O L T N P A B
N J B Y M L H F X B T W N B W R A Q E A
L W F I U Z C T E H C O R C O R C Q M C
```

AIRPLANE	FUN	SELFIES
BUNK BEDS	HOTEL	SHOW AND TELL
CABIN	KNITTING	SNACKS
CANDY	LESSON	STASH
CLASS	MEALS	TEACHER
CROCHET	OVERNIGHT	WEEKEND
DOOR PRIZE	ROAD TRIP	WIP
FRIENDS	ROOMIES	YARN

Word RoundUp 7

FUN & FUNKY

```
A  T  N  F  I  K  P  D  V  E  A  I  N  T  A  R  S  I  A  V
T  X  E  R  A  U  Q  S  Y  N  N  A  R  G  Y  V  O  O  R  G
S  M  S  I  J  X  V  T  R  Z  R  R  E  G  R  U  B  M  A  H
I  B  O  X  B  W  L  Y  P  P  U  P  Q  O  N  Z  Z  S  O  K
G  P  A  S  T  A  E  Z  F  P  O  S  D  C  M  I  N  E  D  B
E  S  Z  C  A  P  I  Z  Z  A  U  C  N  K  N  I  E  O  S  N
S  A  P  U  O  I  M  P  R  S  K  R  H  E  I  W  D  G  H  L
U  F  H  O  O  N  C  I  H  Z  E  Y  G  F  Y  H  Z  U  M  Q
E  F  J  E  X  R  O  I  P  W  Q  N  N  T  G  S  I  I  N  C
R  R  V  E  V  T  X  H  O  T  A  Y  P  E  K  A  C  P  U  C
T  O  Z  S  O  P  N  L  P  R  N  W  G  D  D  I  H  C  R  O
R  N  E  Z  E  Z  F  A  O  X  E  F  Q  J  M  N  Q  X  H  Y
A  M  Z  H  O  O  P  T  H  L  Z  E  F  F  A  R  I  G  U  W
H  L  Y  Q  R  R  N  Y  T  P  R  A  D  N  M  N  P  R  K  W
C  P  X  T  G  R  Y  R  S  S  E  T  A  P  E  S  T  R  Y  G
B  J  E  H  U  K  U  M  I  P  V  L  S  A  B  X  P  J  H  P
Q  R  Z  B  Y  T  V  H  L  O  G  K  E  B  T  J  Y  Y  X  M
```

☐ ☐ ☐ ☐ ☐ ☐ 6 foods to crochet

☐ ☐ ☐ ☐ ☐ 5 trendy yarn colors

☐ ☐ ☐ ☐ 4 animal amigurumi

☐ ☐ ☐ 3 crochet colorwork techniques

☐ ☐ 2 70s-inspired crochet motifs

 Word RoundUp 8

```
┌─────────────────────────────────┐
│  A CRAFTER'S LIFE FOR ME  │
└─────────────────────────────────┘
```

```
G F H A X H X L E T O H G J K R C L C D
R S T J J M M O V I E S E W N R B K E F
C V P Y A R N S H O P S B N E T H T S H
H Q L B K Y Y Z O G I X Y A P T A C E Q
U V S K O O B Q T L R L T W O I X A N T
R T T T D S J T C F O I K G L A E I I H
C Q G E T O U F K N V U F O Y N E X Z J
H A C F P P D D Z E E V R L E R E F A D
M K O J M S A J U W I I C T S W E H G N
E V F A Y U E T J D E I C G T L N V A H
N E F E H O W R I N C S L J E B I E M W
A B E B Z I N I T E C Y Y U R O W Z T Z
L P E U B C W E S S N W G C I L Y R C A
P A T T A A D J X G I T U L N B K C E Z
R P Y U F N K E R K O F H K W R F F M F
I R E O K E L X G F P L J S O S N N O D
A H Y Y Q T Y H M P X S B W L L F G H G
```

☐ ☐ ☐ ☐ ☐ ☐ 6 locations to knit or crochet

☐ ☐ ☐ ☐ ☐ 5 places to find patterns

☐ ☐ ☐ ☐ 4 crafter personality traits

☐ ☐ ☐ 3 synthetic yarns

☐ ☐ 2 drinks to sip

Logic Puzzle 7

VINTAGE PATTERNS

Three online sellers of vintage crochet patterns are having a sale. Using the clues below, match each of the sellers with pattern they have on sale, the year it was written, and the country they run their online shop from.

1. The seller based in Ireland has the Crochet Table Mat pattern on sale.

2. Of the seller from France and Doug, one has the Colorblock Throw pattern and the other, the Newborn Set.

3. The pattern from 1949 isn't from the seller in Ireland.

4. The 1985 pattern, the Newborn Set, and the English seller represent three different listings.

5. The pattern sold by Shawn was written 36 years after the Crochet Table Mat.

6. The Crochet Table Mat pattern wasn't written in 1931.

7. The Gloves pattern is on sale from Shawn.

8. Deanne's sale pattern was written 36 years before the one offered by the Scottish seller.

9. Either Meredith or Shawn is the seller of The Colorblock Throw pattern.

10. Ruby, the seller from England, and the Gloves make up three different listings.

		PATTERN					SELLER					COUNTRY				
		Crochet Table Mat	Lacy Blouse	Gloves	Colorblock Throw	Newborn Set	Doug	Meredith	Ruby	Shawn	Deanne	Denmark	England	France	Ireland	Scotland
YEAR	1913															
	1931															
	1949															
	1967															
	1985															
COUNTRY	Denmark															
	England															
	France															
	Ireland															
	Scotland															
SELLER	Doug															
	Meredith															
	Ruby															
	Shawn															
	Deanne															

YEAR	PATTERN	SELLER	COUNTRY
1913			
1931			
1949			
1967			
1985			

Intermediate

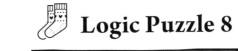 Logic Puzzle 8

STITCH 'N' SNACK

The Madison Knitters Guild has many elder members who meet together with newcomers to practice basic stitches. During the last meetup, each duo also shared a snack while they worked. Match the teacher-student pairing with their meeting time and snack of choice using only the clues below.

1. The student that snacked on toffee has her lesson sometime after Vicky teaches.

2. The newbie that chose toffee, Lindsay, and Darlene's mentee are three different people.

3. Rose scheduled her lesson 3 hours after Pearl's.

4. Lindsay isn't learning knitting from Rose.

5. Of the student that chose pizza and Pearl's mentee, one has the 4:00pm lesson and the other is Mila.

6. Of Pearl's student and Lindsay, one has the 4:00pm meetup and the other munched on Girl Scout cookies.

7. Georgia snacked on bean dip during her lesson.

8. Harriet arrived ready to knit at 5:00pm.

9. Teachers Evelyn and Darlene did not bring Girl Scout cookies.

10. The student that snacked on pizza either had a 6:00pm lesson or learned from Rose.

		Nora	Mila	Greta	Harriet	Lindsay	Darlene	Evelyn	Vicky	Pearl	Rose	Trail mix	Toffee	Pizza	Bean dip	Girl Scout cookies
TIME	4:00 pm															
	5:00 pm															
	6:00 pm															
	7:00 pm															
	8:00 pm															
SNACK	Trail mix															
	Toffee															
	Pizza															
	Bean dip															
	Girl Scout cookies															
TEACHER	Darlene															
	Evelyn															
	Vicky															
	Pearl															
	Rose															

TIME	STUDENT	TEACHER	SNACK
4:00 pm			
5:00 pm			
6:00 pm			
7:00 pm			
8:00 pm			

Crossword Puzzle 8

AROUND THE WORLD

ACROSS

1 knitting style also called "picking"

3 most common knitting style, especially popular in British Isles and North America

6 tiny island producing famous two-color sweaters (2 wds)

9 two-color knits with motif color trapped across the back until it is needed

11 Norwegian knitting tradition known for "lusekofta" or "lice" pattern

14 to survive potato famine, they crocheted for work

15 birthplace of amigurumi

17 geometric designs added to Fair Isle knits

18 tension of the yarn is wrapped around the base of the neck in this world knitting style

19 textured knitting patterns that originated off Ireland's west coast

20 purl stitch country of origin in 16th century

DOWN

1 uses two different sized knitting needles on purpose (2 wds)

2 never turn your work and use an afghan hook to crochet in this style

4 U.S. founding father's wife who knit socks for Rev. War troops (2 wds)

5 type of crochet that resembles fancy granny squares

7 historian Richard Rutt suggests first knitters were these people between 500 and 1200 A.D.

8 19th century royal known for knitting and crochet (2 wds)

10 this knitting style oft employs a special knitting belt to hold working needle against the body

12 International Crochet Day month

13 this knitting style shares its name with a cocktail of vodka, coffee liqueur, and cream served over ice

16 World Wide Knit in Public Day month

 Crossword Puzzle 9

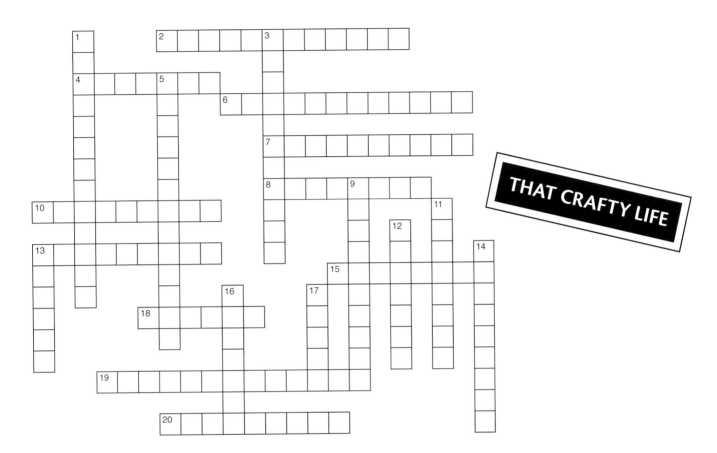

THAT CRAFTY LIFE

ACROSS

2 crafting's dopamine effect (2 wds)

4 online hangout for yarn crafters since 2007

6 monthly meetup of crafters (2 wds)

7 can't yarn shop there on Sunday (2 wds)

8 Famous ones include Jackson or J. Fox

10 chardonnay container (2 wds)

13 deep discount yarn

15 enough yarn for a small project (2 wds)

18 slang for crocheter

19 untapped talent in craft patterns (2 wds)

20 KAL, for short

DOWN

1 striped mittens politician in 2021 meme (2 wds)

3 yarn delivery by post (2 wds)

5 li'l fiber retailer near you (3 wds)

9 sleepless knitting marathon (2 wds)

11 social network known for groups and live video

12 sell or trade unwanted yarn

13 stay-up-late drink

14 mobile app for sharing makes

16 getaway for crafters

17 big box craft retailer HQed Ohio

Word Search 9

YARN COLORS

```
A W Q I E U L B Y V A N B E A P S C O W
N V X V X U Y N E E R G T S E R O F H B
C C Z W V V D K T A N G E R I N E I R N
U O K I B L P K Q L P K E A M V T O D G
P C C I T O I U W Q I A Q M Z E W L P N
F E S O R K A Y M J Y E R E D N E V A L
G P L J J R M E J P G H D M A O F A E S
R M I M E Q E N P I K J B O P N P E P L
O A P N M J E O K R N I J X S L E N O I
L I R M K V F H Z G G Z N Z L Q E I L D
O Z D C E N F T S Y H T E M A M K R A O
C E L A W U O X A Y R S J Q Y U M A N F
I N A I W Q C S R E H C A E P H A M I F
T Z R H R A D R V O R Y K O L O O A D A
L Y E B Q L E L B U R G U N D Y K U R D
U S M M O H I E G G S H E L L L L Q A G
M A E G C S D I H C R O O S A G E A C A
```

AMETHYST	EMERALD	PINK
AQUAMARINE	FOREST GREEN	PEACH
BROWN	GOLD	PUMPKIN
BURGUNDY	HONEY	ROSE
CARDINAL	MAIZE	SAGE
CHERRY	LAVENDER	SEAFOAM
COFFEE	MULTICOLOR	SILVER
DAFFODIL	NAVY BLUE	TANGERINE
EGGSHELL	ORCHID	WHITE

Word Search 10

CRAZY YARN LADY

```
T  K  E  K  Q  E  S  K  E  I  N  E  M  L  A  C  P  E  E  K
I  Q  E  W  E  F  Y  V  Z  K  Y  E  W  H  X  I  C  L  H  Z
M  D  T  R  R  M  S  A  K  M  U  I  Q  L  J  Q  L  S  U  R
E  I  O  E  J  I  O  L  D  F  D  E  S  S  E  S  B  O  G  Z
T  T  W  K  H  I  S  N  Y  L  U  Q  J  P  A  D  E  X  S  Y
O  R  S  O  N  C  I  R  F  S  L  P  I  L  E  V  A  R  N  U
U  K  G  N  O  O  O  Q  E  E  O  A  D  F  P  L  J  R  N  F
N  T  L  W  E  L  T  R  C  D  I  M  T  E  J  O  R  D  O  I
W  G  I  T  E  P  S  D  C  H  R  L  U  E  M  P  J  B  A  S
I  A  S  N  V  D  P  U  I  N  S  A  E  C  H  U  D  L  Z  V
N  N  T  G  K  O  A  A  R  S  O  U  O  R  H  C  S  Y  V  Q
D  R  A  E  W  O  K  M  H  V  T  D  P  H  S  Y  O  N  H  Z
E  A  S  T  N  H  T  J  D  T  I  U  E  K  N  S  A  R  O  J
H  Y  H  A  M  G  P  N  G  N  I  V  R  K  H  R  E  R  C  C
B  T  D  E  G  X  M  J  R  W  A  N  E  B  O  V  A  R  N  A
A  O  O  R  R  E  D  Q  D  O  J  H  K  U  P  O  M  Y  T  T
L  G  X  C  Y  Q  D  V  Z  Y  B  M  F  Y  S  U  H  N  I  S
```

BORN TO KNIT	HOOKED ON CROCHET	SO MUCH YARN
CONSUMED	ISO	STASH
CREATE	I WOOL SURVIVE	STRESS RELIEF
CROCHET ALL DAY	KEEP CALM	TIME TO UNWIND
DO KNOT DISTURB	KNIT HAPPENS	UNRAVEL
GOT YARN	OBSESSED	YARN HOARDER
HANDMADE	SKEIN	

Word Scramble 7

Unscramble the words to find words that match the scramble's theme.

YARN PROJECTS

EBTSOOI _ _ _ _ _ _ _

EWATSRE _ _ _ _ _ _ _

RPESILPS _ _ _ _ _ _ _ _

FCASR _ _ _ _ _

COSKS _ _ _ _ _

NTEISMT _ _ _ _ _ _ _

FIESUTSF _ _ _ _ _ _ _ _

LNBATEK _ _ _ _ _ _ _

TSEORCAS _ _ _ _ _ _ _ _

UEPRS _ _ _ _ _

EBIENA _ _ _ _ _ _

PACE _ _ _ _

ASTKBE _ _ _ _ _ _

TAGBONOG _ _ _ _ _ _ _ _

HMOE RCODE _ _ _ _ _ _ _ _ _

EOTT GBA _ _ _ _ _ _ _

DOSLCITHH _ _ _ _ _ _ _ _ _

ELIRENFSGS
ELGVOS _ _ _ _ _ _ _ _ _ _ _ _ _

RFLOO FOUP _ _ _ _ _ _ _ _ _

EDBDNAAH _ _ _ _ _ _ _ _

UMG YOZC _ _ _ _ _ _ _

REA REMWRSA _ _ _ _ _ _ _ _ _ _

YABB BBI _ _ _ _ _ _ _

FWRIFSE DPA _ _ _ _ _ _ _ _ _ _

ELG MWSRAER _ _ _ _ _ _ _ _ _ _

 Word Scramble 8

Unscramble the words to find words that match the scramble's theme.

BRAND RECOGNITION

ETANRB _ _ _ _ _ _

AMDO ERVA _ _ _ _ _ _ _ _

MTROAUCLR _ _ _ _ _ _ _ _ _

DLAAPSRS _ _ _ _ _ _ _ _

WYNED _ _ _ _ _

TKIAH _ _ _ _ _

ASDCAEC _ _ _ _ _ _ _

CEI SARNY _ _ _ _ _ _ _

REEIPRM _ _ _ _ _ _ _

IOLN ANRDB _ _ _ _ _ _ _ _ _

HMPOTULY _ _ _ _ _ _ _ _

NKTI PKSIC _ _ _ _ _ _ _ _ _

YUPPP _ _ _ _ _

NTASPO _ _ _ _ _ _

DER ETHAR _ _ _ _ _ _ _ _

NAAL SASOGR _ _ _ _ _ _ _ _ _ _

RONAW _ _ _ _ _

Criss Cross 7

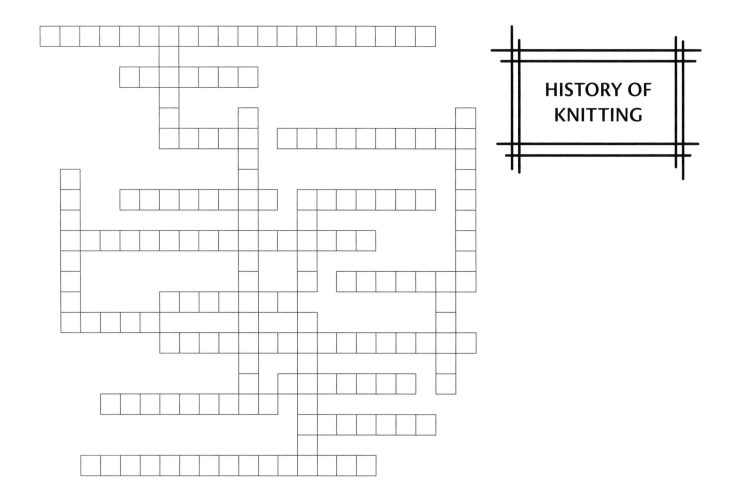

HISTORY OF KNITTING

20 letters

INDUSTRIAL
REVOLUTION

16 letters

MARTHA
WASHINGTON

REVOLUTIONARY
WAR

15 letters

KNITTING MACHINE

QUEEN ELIZABETH I

10 letters

MIDDLE EAST

9 letters

CRAFTSMEN

STOCKINGS

8 letters

FAIR ISLE

GARMENTS

PATRIOTS

7 letters

BOYCOTT

DRESSES

ENGLAND

GIRDLES

IRELAND

SCARVES

6 letters

EUROPE

ROYALS

5 letters

EGYPT

SOCKS

SPAIN

Criss Cross 8

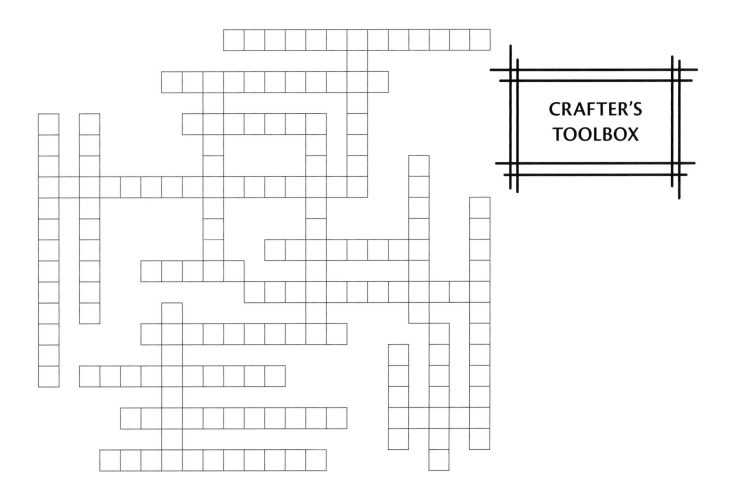

CRAFTER'S TOOLBOX

16 letters
STITCH DICTIONARY

13 letters
DARNING NEEDLE
MEASURING TAPE

12 letters
INSTRUCTIONS
STITCH MARKER

11 letters
BLOCKING MAT
CABLE NEEDLE
SPRAY BOTTLE
TAPERED HOOK

10 letters
BALL WINDER
INLINE HOOK
PROJECT BAG
YARN NEEDLE

8 letters
GLOSSARY
SCISSORS
STOPPERS
YARN BOWL

7 letters
BOBBINS
PATTERN

5 letters
GAUGE
SKEIN
STASH

Word RoundUp 9

GO BIG OR GO HOME

```
A V R N E W Y O R K C I T Y P E Y R B L
M O P Y H N F T N M I E M H C O E D O S
S T M B U L K Y V L F R V J Q Q L S Y X
T I I H T Y Z S B U S T E D D Q A D A F
E N Z N T Y Y Y O A D Y Q Y F N N B I V
R O T B A E F P Q M T R L E G E A N N J
D Y Q V M Q R T J D O R G E Y Q G Y C B
A O T M L O U E U T W N L V R E K M M P
M F T R O N G R A R I E O B R N E L A P
N R F L O K Y L O G S S I S U E B R J L
Z R F D X S U T N P N M T H P F I P W D
X S N V C M C A O I I F C E C S U T B F
W O P U U E H O A U F F H P V R D C J A
L L S C L L C T B B L A N K E T P V H X
O S C L L H R R K M R E L I P K C O T S
O A O A V U T F O Q U V A R M S K G U R
C C W I C C J E K D B J M K D K C I H T
```

☐ ☐ ☐ ☐ ☐ ☐   *6 big cities for yarnies*

☐ ☐ ☐ ☐ ☐   *5 oversize knits for the home*

☐ ☐ ☐ ☐   *4 descriptors for big yarn*

☐ ☐ ☐   *3 yarn hoarder synonyms*

☐ ☐   *2 appendages to craft with*

Word RoundUp 10

NERD OUT ON KNITTING

```
V N O N O W U S P A C O M E H C T B Y H
N Q Z E Y R D Q O X H L Z S N G R H A R
P A P T Y E S E D G A D K Y S B W F S A
S C P T H B L Z T N E U N T U C G S C L
T R U E N E C B O N H P E E U T I N K U
U E L D C I R I A P I K T S I I A A T C
R W L Y E H S R K E N O T H Z R E W M R
T N O A D I I F I A G G P U G V F W D I
L E V V V T M N L N M N I E A I D Y J C
E C E O Q B A B E L G O A E L N A J O P
N K R O H H E S I S M B W H A B O R N B
E P N E O I W A N S E T O G C R U W T B
C B G E M B T W S T E W I N I R O O M S
K D W E N G M W E K R D A R E H E D D U
U V E I N I Q A S C R O L V X Q Q T P M
T R Q O W K L A B A O X E E E G J I N W
P F L V K Y B E C R Q A B T I G T X Z I
```

☐ ☐ ☐ ☐ ☐ ☐   6 stitches

☐ ☐ ☐ ☐ ☐   5 sweater styles

☐ ☐ ☐ ☐   4 needles to try

☐ ☐ ☐   3 ways to cast on

☐ ☐   2 things to knit for charity

 Logic Puzzle 9

KNITTING CRUISE

A group of friends decided to go on a knitting cruise. Using only the clues below, match each person to the number skeins they traveled with, the project they completed, and the shore excursion they took.

1. Sadie brought 2 more skeins than the friend who planned the dice game.

2. Maria is either the knitter who visited a private beach or the person who organized the dice game.

3. The friend who went kayaking didn't plan the secret sister swap.

4. Cherilyn didn't bring exactly 7 skeins.

5. The five people are the person who brought 11 skeins, the person who went hiking at the ruins, Lana, the person who planned Bingo, and the person who planned the secret sister swap.

6. Johanna went hiking at the ruins, and the friend who brought 11 skeins planned morning yoga.

7. The friend who brought 5 skeins went kayaking.

8. The friend who visited a private beach, the knitter who planned karaoke, and Lana are three different people.

9. Sadie went kayaking, and the person who brought 9 skeins planned karaoke.

10. The knitter who brought 3 skeins didn't try swimming with dolphins.

		Maria	Johanna	Lana	Cherilyn	Sadie	Dice game	Secret sister swap	Morning yoga	Karaoke	Bingo	Private beach	Kayaking	Snorkeling	Hiking the ruins	Dolphin swim
SKEINS	3															
	5															
	7															
	9															
	11															
EXCURSION	Private beach															
	Kayaking															
	Snorkeling															
	Hiking the ruins															
	Dolphin swim															
ACTIVITY	Dice game															
	Secret sister swap															
	Morning yoga															
	Karaoke															
	Bingo															

SKEINS	NAME	ACTIVITY	EXCURSION
3			
5			
7			
9			
11			

Logic Puzzle 10

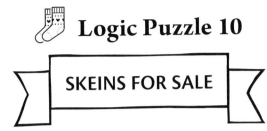

SKEINS FOR SALE

Cozy Yarn Co. received five of wholesale yarn orders this week. Using the clues below, match each customer to the number of skeins ordered, the total price of their order, and the town their order will be shipped to. Note: Due to buyer discounts, the price is not necessarily correlated to the order size.

1. Of the order placed by Whit Royal and the 65 skein order, one cost $550 and the other is going to Boise.

2 The 70 skein order didn't cost $1,500.

3. The $2,000 order is 15 skeins smaller than the order placed by Bev Anderson.

4. Of the $2,000 order and the box going to Columbus, one is 60 skeins and the other was bought by Coreen Spence.

5. The order going to New Castle is 5 skeins smaller than the one bought by Linda Judd.

6. The $1,250 order was either bought by Coreen Spence or contains 65 skeins.

7. The order placed by Linda Judd is going to Danbury.

8. Whit Royal's order is 5 skeins less than the order going to Minneapolis.

9. The order going to New Castle is smaller than Whit Royal's order.

		BUYER					PRICE					TOWN			
		Bev Anderson	Coreen Spence	Randy Detty	Whit Royal	Linda Judd	$550	$920	$1,250	$1,500	$2,000	Minneapolis	Columbus	Boise	New Castle	Danbury
SKEINS	55															
	60															
	65															
	70															
	75															
TOWN	Minneapolis															
	Columbus															
	Boise															
	New Castle															
	Danbury															
PRICE	$550															
	$920															
	$1,250															
	$1,500															
	$2,000															

SKEINS	BUYER	PRICE	TOWN
55			
60			
65			
70			
75			

Crossword Puzzle 10

YARNIE JARGON

ACROSS

5 knit that fits true to size (2 wds)

8 ssk (3 wds)

10 project that's done (2 wds)

12 insane fiber gentlewoman (3 wds)

14 patterns designed to use up leftover yarn

17 PHD (3 wds)

18 holds your WIPs (2 wds)

DOWN

1 hook yarn with one of ten appendages (2 wds)

2 UFO (2 wds)

3 swap needles for upper limbs (2 wds)

4 when variegated yarn colors clump together creating big splotches of color

6 seasonal shift that allows for more turtlenecks (2 wds)

7 one's current craft, abbreviated

9 shorthand for reverse stockinette stitch (3 wds)

11 tells when yarn was colored (2 wds)

12 activism centered around craft

13 small stuffed toys created by crochet

15 knitter's collection of raw materials

16 "stash accumulated beyond life expectancy"

Crossword Puzzle 11

STITCHES TO KNOW

ACROSS

3 in crochet, knot of yarn under top two loops of each stitch

6 unraveling your knitting

8 stitch for Eggo lover

9 hide crochet tails with random sewing (3 wds)

12 do again

13 groom tosses it

17 DNA has a double _____

18 small embryonic plant

19 first stitch of your cast on row (2 wds)

20 Adam, to Eve? (2 wds)

21 knit this stitch, a.k.a. twisted

22 lever knitting

DOWN

1 knit one row and purl the next (2 wds)

2 warming up knits with fleece or roving yarn, as in mittens

4 leading leg of yarn on the left of your needle

5 stitch for Longaberger

7 column of knit stitches

9 knit a stitch without any increasing or decreasing (2 wds)

10 falls off the needle (2 wds)

11 can be coil or foam

14 flip crochet over before starting next row

15 move a knit stitch to another needle without working it (2 wds)

16 the start of crochet in the round

Word Search 11

PROJECT PERFECT

```
R Z C G R O C E R Y T O T E Y P Z W C G
L G M S K C O S H R E V O C W O L L I P
Y C M I P T E K N A L B L F Z O T A H V
B W P D T N Y E M K N C V H S N V K L Q
Z K I I S T A X U H P L V A Q E K N X J
A Z X S E U E U B X C Q T U A T R J C H
M S C H I M O N Y O J C O A S T E R S T
F C X C F H J B S G H B O O K M A R K S
D R P L F V K S R E M R A W G E L G R E
O O K O U S X I L N M Y I Y V L T R B V
O C Z T T N D G C G T J M R Y Y N O O D
F E L H S U T T U F R O Z A E K E S E Y
Y D P U N D E R P A N T S H B T M E I V
A E U R X K G L B A B Y G I F T A S X L
L M M O S U W G L O V E S P E V N E G Y
P O K A M O Q L W O B T I U R F R Z W B
U H B Z C A G D N A B D A E H Q O Z H S
```

BABY GIFT	FRUIT BOWL	MITTENS	SATCHEL
BASKET	GLOVES	MUG RUG	SOCKS
BLANKET	GROCERY TOTE	ORNAMENT	STUFFIES
BOOKMARK	HAT	PILLOW COVER	SWEATER
COASTERS	HEADBAND	PLAY FOOD	UNDERPANTS
COWL	HOME DECOR	ROSES	VEST
DISHCLOTH	LEG WARMERS		

🐑 Word Search 12

OH DARN!

```
T S B Z D U I W H A H N O I T C E R I D
D O X W I L Q S R O E G U A G G N O R W
R T O D V W A R W O J H T O U K H T C U
O B I T S Y F D F I N P A W R S K O M D
P A W N I C D R D F S G U N I G T Q H R
P C N T K G O F O E W S W C S S K O I U
E K O R A I H W U G R Z D A K F T P N C
D W E U E N N T M N G I R A Y E O E K K
S A K J N T G G J G S I N V R U R R D M
T R O V Q T T L S O M T N G T N O S I D
I D T E L T I A E W G J I G D W I S V F
T S J F W N W N P D U S E T R O T N E I
C N Y A J R J L G V I X G O C A W W G M
H A C T O I K I L P Q W L T K H R N Q Y
A R W R I U I L A J B O T E Y V L F X J
V T R P C V W Y W Q C A I E R R A T A R
U E A L I F E L I N E L F U K A D K S E
```

BACKWARDS	FIT	PATTERN	TOO TIGHT
COLORWORK	FROGGING	PUCKERS	TWISTED
COUNTING	JOGS	RIP OUT	UH OH
DIRECTION	KNOTS	SWISS DARNING	UNSTITCH
DROPPED STITCH	LADDERING DOWN	TANGLED	WRONG GAUGE
ERRATA	LIFELINE	TINKING	WRONG WAY
ERROR	MISTAKE		

Word Mine 7

See how many words you can make out of the letters in popular yarn types!

┌─ YARN TYPES ─┐
MOHAIR

5-letter words (2)	4-letter words (11)	3-letter words (25)		2-letter words (15)
_ _ _ _ _	_ _ _ _	_ _ _	_ _ _	_ _
_ _ _ _ _	_ _ _ _	_ _ _	_ _ _	_ _
	_ _ _ _	_ _ _	_ _ _	_ _
	_ _ _ _	_ _ _	_ _ _	_ _
	_ _ _ _	_ _ _	_ _ _	_ _
	_ _ _ _	_ _ _	_ _ _	_ _
	_ _ _ _	_ _ _	_ _ _	_ _
	_ _ _ _	_ _ _	_ _ _	_ _
	_ _ _ _	_ _ _	_ _ _	_ _
	_ _ _ _	_ _ _	_ _ _	_ _
	_ _ _ _	_ _ _	_ _ _	_ _
		_ _ _	_ _ _	_ _
		_ _ _		_ _
				_ _
				_ _

Solutions

Logic Puzzle Sample—DOGGIE COATS

DOG	OUTERWEAR	AGE
Rufus	Cable-knit sweater	10
King	Wool socks	7
Sadie	Reindeer hoodie	8
Chloe	Snowflake hat	9

Crossword Puzzle 1—SWEATER WEATHER

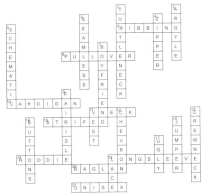

Word Search 1—AMIGURUMI

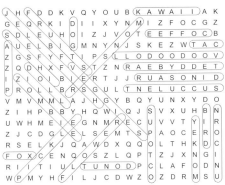

Word Search 2—CELEBS WHO KNIT OR CROCHET

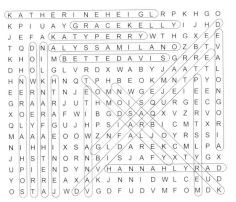

Word Scramble 1—KNITTER'S GLOSSARY

PATTERN
SATIN STITCH
CAST ON
BEGIN
FRONT LOOP

CABLE NEEDLE
YARN OVER
FROGGING
REPEAT
ALTERNATE

PURL
GARTER STITCH
BAR INCREASE
CHANNEL
ROW
WRONG SIDE

RIGHT SIDE
BUTTONHOLE
BIND OFF
SLIP STITCH
TENSION

Word Scramble 2—KNITTING TERMS

SLIPKNOT
FOLLOW
DECREASE
REVERSE
CONTINUE
PICK UP
BETWEEN

INCREASE
LOOP
BIAS
NEEDLE
MAIN COLOR
INVISIBLE
SEAM

CONTRAST
COLOR
WRAP AND
TURN
PLACE
MARKER
STOCKINETTE
STITCH

KNITWISE
PURLWISE
WORK EVEN
BACKSTITCH
BLANKET
STITCH

Criss Cross 1—PLACES TO KNIT OR CROCHET

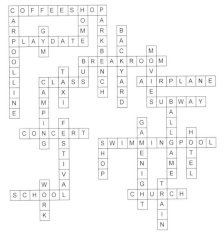

Criss Cross 2—GUILD MEETING

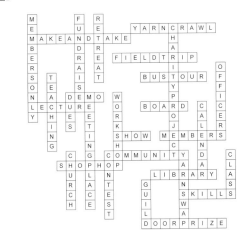

Word RoundUp 1—CRAFT IT CUTE

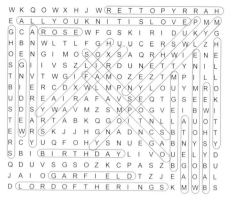

Word RoundUp 2—SOPHISTICATED STYLE

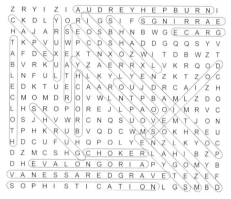

Logic Puzzle 1—SHOPPING FUN

SHOPPER	SPENT	FORGOT
Peggy	$35	Variegated Yarn
Suzy	$45	Needles
Jean	$25	Crochet Hook
Becca	$15	Pattern

Logic Puzzle 2—MISSING HOOKS

PIECES	PATTERN	QUILTER
Bernie	6	Bronze
Alice	10	Silver
Ronny	8	Bamboo
Olivia	4	Pink

Word Mine 1—PLANT

4-letter words (3)	PAT	LA
PANT	APT	NA
PLAN	LAP	PA
PLAT	LAT	TA
3-letter words (12)	TAP	
ALP	NAP	AL
ALT	PAL	AN
	PAN	AT
	TAN	
	2-letter words (7)	

Word Mine 2—COTTON

5-letter words (1)	TOOT	OOT
CONTO	3-letter words (10)	TON
4-letter words (7)	CON	TOO
COON	COO	TOT
COOT	COT	2-letter words (3)
ONTO	NOO	NO
OTTO	NOT	ON
TOCO	ONO	TO
TOON		

Crossword Puzzle 2—KNIT-TERMINOLOGY

Crossword Puzzle 3—CROCHET, YOU SAY?

Word Search 3—MEASUREMENTS

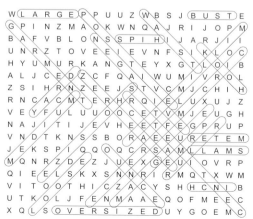

Word Search 4—YARN BRANDS

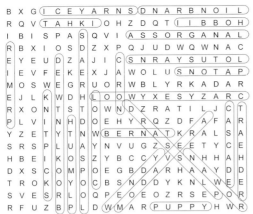

```
B X G I C E Y A R N S D N A R B N O I L
R Q V T A H K I O H Z D Q T I I B B O H
I B I S P A S Q V I A S S O R G A N A L
R B X I O S D Z X P Q J U D W Q W N A C
E Y E U D Z A J I C S N R A Y S U T O L
I E V F E K E X J A W O L U S N O T A P
M O S W E E G R U O R W B L Y R K A D A R
E J L K W D H L O O W Y X E S Y Z A R C
R X O N T S T O W N D Z R A T I L J C T
P L V I N H D O E H Y R Q Z D F A F A R
Y Z E T Y Y T N W B E R N A T K R A L S A
S R S P L U A Y N V U G Z S E E T Y C E
H B E I K O S Z Y B C C Y V S N H H A H
D X S C O M P O E G B D A R H A A Y D D
T R O K O Y O C B S N D D Y K N L W E E
S V E S R L O Q P E O E O Z R S E P O R
R F U Z B P L D W M A R P U P P Y H W R
```

Word Scramble 3—CRAFT EVERYWHERE

- SUBWAY
- PLAYDATE
- GAME NIGHT
- SCHOOL
- MOVIES
- CARPOOL LINE
- CHURCH
- BALL GAME
- PARK BENCH
- TRAIN
- HOTEL
- CAMPING
- BREAK ROOM
- HOME
- RETREAT
- TAXI
- VACATION
- SWIMMING POOL
- COFFEE SHOP
- BACKYARD
- AIRPORT

Word Scramble 4—CROCHET TERMS 1

- SEAMING
- BLOCKING
- HOOK
- POST
- WRAPPING
- INCREASE
- FASTEN OFF
- AFGHAN
- TASSEL
- TURN
- BRAID
- TIE OFF
- SLIP KNOT
- TAPERED HOOK
- MESH STITCH
- PICOT STITCH
- GRANNY SQUARE
- INLINE HOOK
- POPCORN STITCH
- WORKING YARN
- FINGER CROCHET
- JOINING SQUARES
- HALF DOUBLE CROCHET
- BERRY STITCH
- BACK LOOPS
- TURNING CHAIN

Criss Cross 3—KNIT STYLE

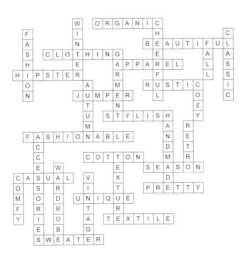

```
        W   O R G A N I C
  F     I       B E A U T I F U L   C
F A S H I O N   E               A   A
  H   C L O T H I N G   A P P A R E L   S
  I   P S T E R   A           L   O   S
  O       N   A   M   R U S T I C   Z   I
  N       J U M P E R   N           O   C
          T   A       S T Y L I S H   A
  F A S H I O N A B L E       A       R
  C       U           C O T T O N   E
  E   W   M           E       S E A S O N
C A S U A L           V       D
O   O             U N I Q U E   P R E T T Y
M   R             D   R
F   I             U   A
Y   E             T   G
  S W E A T E R
```

Criss Cross 4—ALL THE FEELS

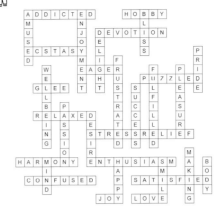

```
A D D I C T E D       H O B B Y
  M   U           N       O
  U   S           J   D E V O T I O N
E C S T A S Y     O       L
  E   D           M       S
      W       E A G E R   F     P
      E       N   H   U   P U Z Z L E D
    G L E E   T   U   S   L     I
      L   B   H   S   T   F     D
      R E L A X E D   R   I     E
      N   S   S   I   A   L     D
      I   S       A   C
      O           S   T R E S S R E L I E F
H A R M O N Y   E N T H U S I A S M     M
      D                           A   K   B
    C O N F U S E D       S A T I S F I E D
      D               P           L   N
              J O Y   L O V E         G
```

Word RoundUp 3—YARN KNOWLEDGE

```
U L H C N I S R L O D K E R E M H S A C
V O B A N Z E A E E O O O B M A B F W
S C E I N C V M I D E C F R M T A Z F W
V L N X C P O Q P J G E T D N P L I Y
U Y A T M I G R K R S I A R E T E M
J A T O V P L Y A J E A G R G O Q R W
D R P S T A Z Y Q C V T X L T H N F T I
A S K V B O L J C H O L M Q G N A C
R H K W O N D J E S A K N H I W O O O V
B O G A B S S Z T S T I N D K T Y W G E
P I N B F T W F S R L A R Q N O N P
O A Q L L P Q O R G M A L M W A L E S O
I A X N E K O N R G N N T C Y O Y G C B
L H U U E L C H A P C Z C D J B R U I O
```

Word RoundUp 4—CROCHET TO KNOW

```
F A D P L H E A D B A N D E C J P K Y U
R F R T V T S G C Y M N A I R A V A B L
E E V V J S B Y R P G B J L F Z U W W
T M S P B G C Z T H O F G R U A O Y B I
A A S T C M O O I H C G T M U E Q Z I
E K O B Y C N N T K G H U A U E S I
W K E A P E P B I H M D E L E S D N G
S E R U I C R B X C V Q E M T Y P C E U
C L C Q A G T U N I S I A N K H R E V Y
A D R S C D X G S E N S E P Q E O B R P
R E E N F F C W Q A R E L S A M U O X E
F E V A U U R F X O E S R S A S U T K C
S N N R W J S W T L H E C C E R A E V
I R A S R X I U N U B Q B P R P I C D C
F A A O M C Z C D O F W U N A N K R E R
Z Y Y B S D N E N I E V A E W T T N S D
```

Logic Puzzle 3—KNITTING SISTERS

NAME	SKEINS	MONTH
Eileen	5	February
Fay	6	June
Sonia	4	April
Rhonda	3	September

Logic Puzzle 4—MAGAZINE HOARDER

NATIONALITY	PATTERN COUNT	PRICE
Canadian	6	$8.50
British	10	$7
Icelandic	8	$5.50
Australian	4	$10

Word Mine 3—RAYON

4-letter words (3)
NARY
ROAN
YARN

3-letter words (10)
ANY
NAY
NOR
OAR
ORA
RAN
RAY
RYA

YAR
YON

2-letter words (10)
AN
AR
AY
NA

NO
ON
OR
OY
YA
YO

Word Mine 4—BAMBOO

5-letter word (1)
BABOO

4-letter words (5)
AMBO
BOBO
BOMB

BOOB
BOOM

3-letter words (9)
BAM
BOA
BOB
BOO

MOA
MOB
MOO
OBA
OMA

2-letter words (7)
AB

AM
BA
BO
MA
MO
OM

Crossword Puzzle 4—TOOLS OF THE TRADE

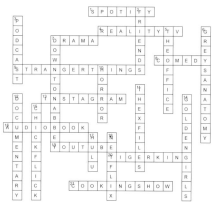

Crossword Puzzle 5—KNIT-TERTAINMENT

Word Search 5—EXOTIC PLACES TO KNIT

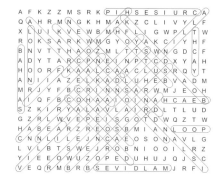

Word Search 6—CRAFT-WORTHY OCCASIONS

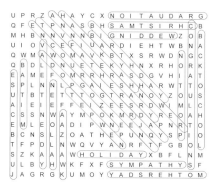

Word Scramble 5—CROCHET TERMS 2

WHIPSTITCH SEAM
MAGIC RING
DROP STITCH
IN THE ROUND
SHELL STITCH
STITCH MARKER

GAUGE
YARN OVER
CHAIN
DOUBLE CROCHET
CAMEL STITCH
TUNISIAN CROCHET

SINGLE CROCHET
THUMB REST
SLIP STITCH
TAIL
TOP LOOPS
TRIPLE CROCHET

THIRD LOOP
TENSION
YARN NEEDLE
DECREASE
WEAVE IN ENDS

Word Scramble 6—TYPES OF YARN

HEMP
ARAN
CHUNKY
LINEN
VARIEGATED

ALPACA
SUPERWASH WOOL
ACRYLIC
PLARN

WORSTED
MOHAIR
WOOL
COTTON
SPORT

MERINO
ANGORA
SYNTHETIC
HOMESPUN
SILK

BAMBOO
ROVING
NATURAL
VEGAN
CASHMERE

Criss Cross 5—ULTIMATE KNITTING SPACE

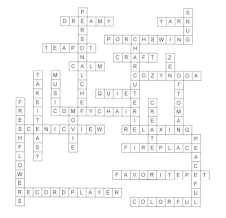

🧶 Criss Cross 6—CROCHET ALL DAY

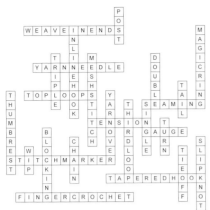

🧦 Logic Puzzle 6—TV TIME

EPISODES	KNITTER	SHOW	DAY
2	Karen	*Gilmore Girls*	Friday
3	Alex	*This Is Us*	Sunday
4	Mindy	*Game of Thrones*	Saturday
5	Paola	*Handmaid's Tale*	Tuesday

🤟 Word Mine 5—ACRYLIC

6-letter word (1)		3-letter words (15)	
RACILY	ARIL	AIL	RAY
5-letter words (5)	ARYL	AIR	RIA
	CARL	ARC	RYA
CIRCA	CLAY	CAR	YAR
CLARY	LACY	CAY	**2-letter words (7)**
LAIRY	LAIC	CRY	
LYRIC	LAIR	ICY	AI
RIYAL	LARI	LAC	AL
4-letter words (15)	LIAR	LAR	AR
	LIRA	LAY	AY
ACYL	RACY	RAI	LA
AIRY	RAIL		LI
	RIAL		YA

🤟 Word Mine 6—ANIMAL

6-letter words (2)		3-letter words (16)	
LAMINA	ALMA	AAL	NIL
MANILA	AMIA	AIL	NIM
5-letter words (8)	AMIN	AIM	**2-letter words (11)**
AMAIN	ANAL	AIN	
AMNIA	ANIL	ALA	AA
ANIMA	LAIN	AMA	AI
LAMIA	LAMA	AMI	AL
LANAI	LIMA	ANA	AM
LIANA	LIMN	ANI	AN
LIMAN	MAIL	LAM	IN
MANIA	MAIN	LIN	LA
4-letter words (16)	MANA	MAN	LI
	MINA	MIL	MA
ALAN	NAIL		MI
	NALA		NA
	NAM		

🟦 Word RoundUp 5—KNIT KNOW-HOW

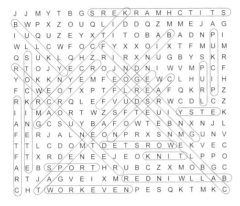

🟦 Word RoundUp 6—WISH LIST

🧦 Logic Puzzle 5—PDF PATTERNS

MONTH	PATTERN	DESIGNER	DOWNLOADS
March	Arm-Knit Pouf	Patty Purl	3.1 million
April	Crochet Cowl	Crafty Chic	6.8 million
May	1-Hour Scarf	Cat Lady Knits	4.2 million
June	Baby Bunny	Amazing Art	1.5 million

🧶 Crossword Puzzle 6—WHAT TO MAKE

Crossword Puzzle 7—CHOOSING YARN

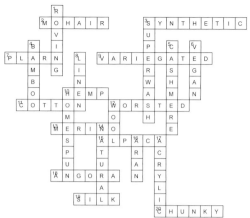

Word RoundUp 8—A CRAFTER'S LIFE FOR ME

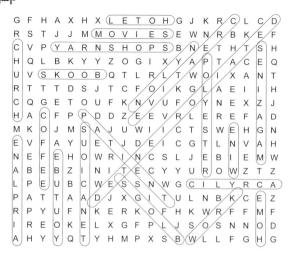

Word Search 7—GET SOCIAL

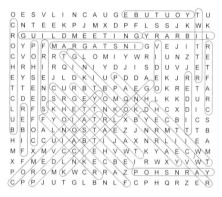

Logic Puzzle 7—VINTAGE PATTERNS

YEAR	PATTERN	SELLER	COUNTRY
1913	Crochet Table Mat	Ruby	Ireland
1931	Lacy Blouse	Deanne	England
1949	Gloves	Shawn	Denmark
1967	Newborn Set	Doug	Scotland
1985	Colorblock Throw	Meredith	France

Word Search 8—GROUP GETAWAYS & RETREATS

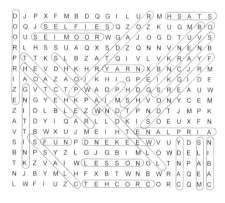

Logic Puzzle 8—STITCH 'N' SNACK

TIME	STUDENT	TEACHER	SNACK
4:00 pm	Greta	Pearl	Bean dip
5:00 pm	Harriet	Darlene	Trail mix
6:00 pm	Lindsay	Vicky	Girl Scout cookies
7:00 pm	Mila	Rose	Pizza
8:00 pm	Nora	Evelyn	Toffee

Word RoundUp 7—FUN & FUNKY

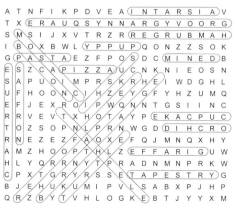

Crossword Puzzle 8—AROUND THE WORLD

Crossword Puzzle 9—THAT CRAFTY LIFE

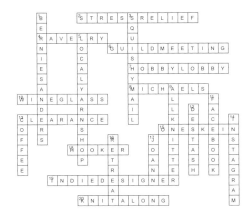

Word Scramble 8—BRAND RECOGNITION

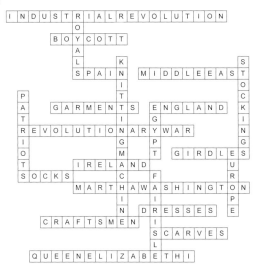

BERNAT	PUPPY	ICE YARNS
CLOURMART	RED HEART	LION BRAND
WENDY	ROWAN	KNIT PICKS
CASCADE	MODA VERA	PATONS
PREMIER	PLASSARD	LANA GROSSA
PLYMOUTH	TAHKI	

Word Search 9—YARN COLORS

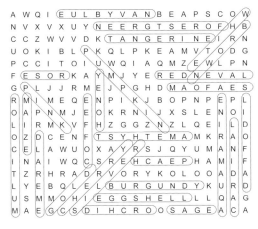

Criss Cross 7—HISTORY OF KNITTING

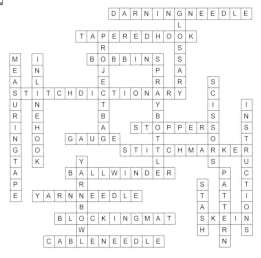

Word Search 10—CRAZY YARN LADY

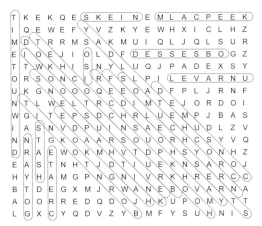

Criss Cross 8—CRAFTER'S TOOLBOX

Word Scramble 7—YARN PROJECTS

BOOTIES	BLANKET	HOME DECOR	MUG COZY
SWEATER	COASTERS	TOTE BAG	EAR WARMERS
SLIPPERS	PURSE	DISHCLOTH	BABY BIB
SCARF	BEANIE	FINGERLESS GLOVES	SWIFFER PAD
SOCKS	CAPE		LEG WARMERS
MITTENS	BASKET	FLOOR POUF	
STUFFIES	TOBOGGAN	HEADBAND	

Word RoundUp 9—GO BIG OR GO HOME

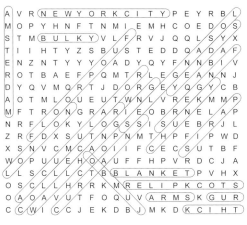

Word RoundUp 10—NERD OUT ON KNITTING

Crossword Puzzle 11—STITCHES TO KNOW

Logic Puzzle 9—KNITTING CRUISE

SKEINS	NAME	ACTIVITY	EXCURSION
3	Lana	Dice game	Snorkeling
5	Sadie	Bingo	Kayaking
7	Maria	Secret sister swap	Private beach
9	Johanna	Karaoke	Hiking the ruins
11	Cherilyn	Morning yoga	Dolphin swim

Word Search 11—PROJECT PERFECT

Logic Puzzle 10—SKEINS FOR SALE

SKEINS	BUYER	PRICE	TOWN
55	Coreen Spence	$1,250	Columbus
60	Randy Detty	$2,000	New Castle
65	Linda Judd	$550	Danbury
70	Whit Royal	$920	Boise
75	Bev Anderson	$1,500	Minneapolis

Word Search 12—OH DARN!

Crossword Puzzle 10—YARNIE JARGON

Word Mine 7—MOHAIR

5-letter words (2)
IHRAM
MOIRA

4-letter words (11)
AMIR
HAIR
HARM
HOAR
HOMA
HORA
MAIR
MORA
OHIA
RAMI
ROAM

3-letter words (25)
AHI
AIM
AIR
AMI
ARM
HAM
HAO
HIM
HOM
MAR
MHO
MIR
MOA
MOR
OAR
OHM
OMA
ORA
RAH
RAI
RAM
RHO
RIA
RIM
ROM

2-letter words (15)
AH
AI
AM
AR
HA
HI
HM
HO
MA
MI
MO
OH
OI
OM
OR